Aces and Places

By the same author:

Bid Boldly, Play Safe

Aces and Places

The International Bridge Circuit

Rixi Markus

SECKER & WARBURG
LONDON

First published in England 1972 by
Martin Secker & Warburg Limited
14 Carlisle Street, London W1V 6NN

Copyright © Rixi Markus 1972

SBN: 436 27325 X

Text set in 11/12 pt. Monotype Times New Roman, printed by
letterpress, and bound in Great Britain at The Pitman Press, Bath

Contents

My friend Derek Senior, Features
Editor of the *Guardian*, has helped
me to select and edit the material
in this book, for which I am
extremely grateful

Foreword

As a child I often dreamed of travelling to all the far countries in the world, and each year during that time I was offered a vacation with friends or relations in various Central European countries as a reward for a good school report. I used to say: "When I grow up I will work hard and make a lot of money to spend on travelling."

In recent years my dreams have become reality. The explanation is that bridge has turned into a popular international sport. Like the sponsors of tennis and golf tournaments, the organisers of bridge festivals all over the world are keen to attract master players to draw the crowds, and I have been lucky enough to be included. At these festivals anyone can join in the fun, seeing interesting places, enjoying bridge competitions, winning prizes and meeting the greatest and most famous players in the bridge world.

The circle of participants has grown considerably. A thousand players assembled at the Palais Chaillot in Paris to compete for a golden trophy and two Renault cars in the biggest bridge event Europe has ever seen – a pairs championship – which was held in July 1971 to honour the memory of the great Cino del Duca, who had a passion for bridge. His widow helped to organise this fantastic event.

The real fun starts when one spends a whole week or even longer with people who have the same interests. Bridge can become a common bond: you play, you discuss bridge incidents and accidents, and when the game is over there is a lot of general relaxation. Would you suspect that Giorgio Belladonna, of the Italian Blue Team, can sing and is a wonderful dancer? Or that his team-mate Garozzo is much keener to win a table-tennis tournament than the bridge trophy in the Algarve? Or that Bob Slavenburg and Roger Trezel win trophies at tennis, and Egmont von Dewitz and

Prince Lichtenstein are also very keen; that Count Fabricotti plays the piano and a good game of golf, and that José le Dentu is a master swimmer? Harold Franklin does everything with passion, and if Leeds United lose a match you had better avoid meeting him that day. Lunch with Terence Reese during the Deauville Bridge Festival, and you will hear about nothing but drives and putts.

All this you can see for yourself while you travel and play tournament bridge. Bridge players are human beings; they can be very amusing away from the table and most of the great ones are charming and polite even while they are concentrating on their job. A further attraction of this bridge travel is the fact that one is offered favourable terms at luxury hotels. Yet another is that the prizes often go down to 30th or 40th place. There are even special prizes for "unseeded" players who achieve honourable positions.

Now I will try to take you with me on my bridge travels.

January

St Moritz

For the last twenty years I have spent three or four weeks
each January in St Moritz and there can be no more invigorat-
ing way to shuffle off the dark December days and the pres-
sures of the old year. The beautiful scenery, the clean air,
the joys of winter sports and the glorious sunshine all com-
bine to give me such a tremendous sense of well-being.
All the hotels provide excellent accommodation; my personal
choice for the first holiday of the year is Suvretta House,
where I feel very much at home. The early part of the day I
spend on the ski slopes – with perhaps more energy than
skill – and then in the late afternoon, physically tired but
mentally alert, I am more than ready to sit down at the bridge
table in the glamorous Palace Hotel.

There are many well-known bridge players and many
well-known people who play bridge. In St Moritz it is more
often the latter group that brings the excitement of the white
slopes outdoors to the green baize indoors. The bidding is,
to say the least, unorthodox at times, but competition is
fierce and the play of the cards often excellent. Inspired
"views" are the order of the day, as these two hands which
I watched well illustrate. The four players concerned were
Peter Adam, a successful London businessman, Henri
Plessner from Paris, Isidore Kerman, a brilliant London
lawyer, and The Right Hon. Harold Lever MP – better

1

known as the Brain of Britain. On the first hand South (Harold Lever) dealt at game all:

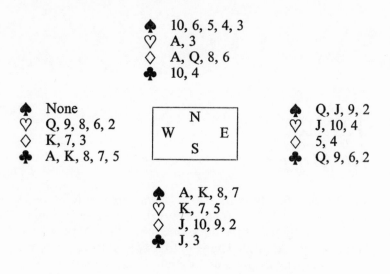

```
                    ♠  10, 6, 5, 4, 3
                    ♡  A, 3
                    ◇  A, Q, 8, 6
                    ♣  10, 4

♠  None                              ♠  Q, J, 9, 2
♡  Q, 9, 8, 6, 2         N            ♡  J, 10, 4
◇  K, 7, 3          W        E        ◇  5, 4
♣  A, K, 8, 7, 5         S            ♣  Q, 9, 6, 2

                    ♠  A, K, 8, 7
                    ♡  K, 7, 5
                    ◇  J, 10, 9, 2
                    ♣  J, 3
```

South opened the bidding with 1♠, West doubled and North raised to 4♠, which became the final contract.

West cashed the king and ace of clubs and continued with a low heart. It seemed likely on the bidding that the king of diamonds was with West and that he would be short in trumps. So declarer decided to test the diamonds first. He won the heart lead in hand, led the 9 of diamonds and ran it when West did not cover. Had the diamond finesse lost he would have had no recourse but to play out the two top trumps hoping for a 2–2 break. But now that the diamond finesse seemed proven he could afford to, and did, make the correct safety play of the 7 of spades from hand in order to limit his trump losses to one.

And here is the other hand with Henri Plessner sitting South. It was game all, each side had a part-score and West dealt:

2

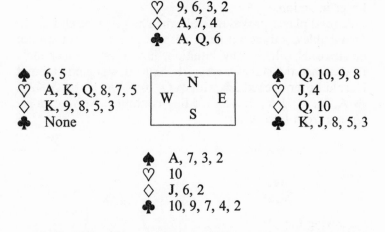

♠ K, J, 4
♡ 9, 6, 3, 2
◇ A, 7, 4
♣ A, Q, 6

♠ 6, 5
♡ A, K, Q, 8, 7, 5
◇ K, 9, 8, 5, 3
♣ None

♠ Q, 10, 9, 8
♡ J, 4
◇ Q, 10
♣ K, J, 8, 5, 3

♠ A, 7, 3, 2
♡ 10
◇ J, 6, 2
♣ 10, 9, 7, 4, 2

The bidding was as crisp as the snow outside. West opened 1♡, North doubled and East bid 1NT. South passed, West tried 2◇ and North doubled again. This time East redoubled and South decided to bid 3♣. When this came round to East he doubled so confidently that we were afraid he would start an avalanche.

West led the king of hearts followed by the ace, which declarer ruffed. With some idea of obtaining two entries to dummy via the spade finesse in order to ruff two more hearts in his own hand, he led a low spade and played the jack from table. East won with the queen and continued with the 10 of spades, won in dummy with the king. Declarer now led another spade to his ace and ruffed his fourth spade in dummy. Next came a low heart, and East was struggling in a drift. Finally he decided to ruff with the jack of trumps, South discarded a diamond and East switched to the queen of diamonds. The ace in dummy took the trick and the last heart was led. East, now in panic, ruffed with the king (instead of discarding his diamond) and had to lead a club to dummy's ace when South discarded his last diamond. A diamond was ruffed in hand, dummy entered with the queen of clubs and another diamond ruff gave declarer his doubled contract.

Here is an even more characteristic example of Harold Lever in action.

A good player proves his skill when he gets himself into an unmakable contract but never despairs; more often than not he succeeds, whether by intuition, ingenuity or sheer luck. In this case the stakes were fairly high: it was game all and Harold Lever opened 2♣ with ♠ Q, 10; ♡ A, 10, 6; ◇ K, 9; ♣ A, K, Q, J, 6, 5. The bidding continued without interference from East–West:

South	North
2♣	3◇[1]
4♣	4♡
4♠[2]	6♣

[1] Showing the ace.
[2] Hoping to avoid a spade lead.

This bidding sounds slightly unorthodox, but at the rubber-bridge table players often value their hands with greater optimism than do the scientists at duplicate bridge.

Having got there, and getting a favourable lead, Harold Lever found the only way to make this "unmakable" slam contract:

```
                  ♠  J, 9
                  ♡  K, J, 4, 2
                  ◇  A, 7, 3, 2
                  ♣  10, 9, 8

♠  K, 6, 5, 4, 3, 2      N        ♠  A, 8, 7
♡  8, 3             W         E   ♡  Q, 9, 7, 5
◇  J, 6, 5, 4           S        ◇  Q, 10, 8
♣  2                             ♣  7, 4, 3

                  ♠  Q, 10
                  ♡  A, 10, 6
                  ◇  K, 9
                  ♣  A, K, Q, J, 6, 5
```

West led the 8 of hearts, declarer played the 2 from dummy and East played the 5. In spite of this favourable lead there were still two spade losers – unless South found the only possible solution. If East held four hearts to the queen and one or both of the missing spade honours the contract could be made by stripping the defenders of their diamonds so as to achieve the desired end position. Accordingly, declarer played the ace and king of diamonds, ruffed a low diamond with the jack of trumps, entered dummy with the 10 of trumps, ruffed the last diamond high and cashed the rest of his trumps to reach the following position:

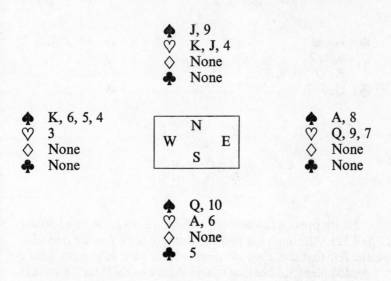

When declarer played the last trump from his own hand West discarded a low spade and declarer discarded the 9 of spades from dummy. East was now in real trouble and he could not save his side. He discarded the ace of spades. Declarer then cashed the ace of hearts and played the queen of spades. West took the trick with the king and had only spades left. South therefore made his 10 of spades and his slam contract.

At competitive bridge, and particularly at pairs scoring, where a difference of a mere 10 points can be important, "views" can be taken in the bidding which would make a confirmed rubber-bridge veteran's hair stand on end. On the following hand Fritzi Gordon was sitting South and North dealt at North–South game:

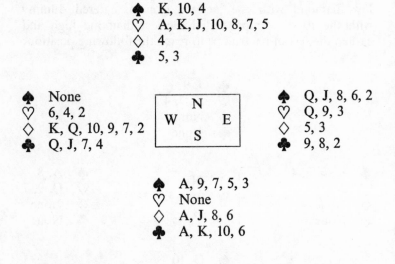

North opened the bidding with 1♡, East passed and South bid 1♠. Although she had the strength for a forcing response she felt that this type of hand, with a void in partner's suit, needed plenty of bidding space. West bid 2NT, the "Unusual No-Trump", asking for his partner's best minor, and a sillier example I have rarely seen, as you will gather from the rest of the auction. North rebid his hearts, East passed and South tried 4♣ – not with any intention of playing there, of course, as clubs had in effect been shown by West, but with the hope of getting spade support from partner. This was duly forthcoming, and when East doubled North's 4♠ bid

South gratefully passed, thankful that the opposition had kept her out of an obviously doomed slam.

Against South's contract of 4♠ doubled West led the king of diamonds. South won with the ace, played the ace and king of clubs and ruffed a club. Two diamonds were discarded on the ace and king of hearts and a low heart ruffed in hand. Declarer now ruffed a diamond with the 10 of spades and led a heart from dummy. This was the position:

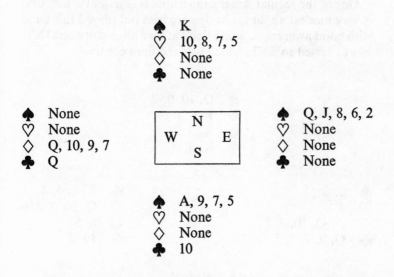

```
                    ♠  K
                    ♡  10, 8, 7, 5
                    ◇  None
                    ♣  None

♠  None                                    ♠  Q, J, 8, 6, 2
♡  None              N                      ♡  None
◇  Q, 10, 9, 7    W     E                   ◇  None
♣  Q                 S                      ♣  None

                    ♠  A, 9, 7, 5
                    ♡  None
                    ◇  None
                    ♣  10
```

It seemed obvious from the double that East held all the trumps and, sure enough, he had to ruff the heart, choosing the jack. Declarer overruffed and then trumped her losing club with the king of spades, the unfortunate East having to part with a low trump. Another heart from dummy, East played a low trump and South overruffed with the 9, surrendering the last two tricks to East's trumps, but making eleven tricks in her doubled contract. The East–West bidding had certainly been a helpful signpost both in the choice of the final contract and in the sequence of play.

7

The "Unusual No-Trump" is one of the conventions that I never agree to play with any but the best players, because it is a dangerous gadget and needs very careful handling.

As can be imagined, rubber bridge at St Moritz is a hotch-potch of systems. I never did decide whether my partner was joking when I asked "Do you play the Unusual No-Trump?" and he replied "No, I'm quite normal."

One of the regular American visitors is Chester Parker, who is very modest about his bridge prowess but played this hand with good awareness. South dealt at love all and opened 1NT. North raised to 3NT, which was the final contract.

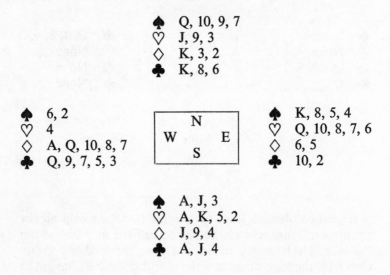

        ♠ Q, 10, 9, 7
        ♡ J, 9, 3
        ◇ K, 3, 2
        ♣ K, 8, 6

♠ 6, 2   ♠ K, 8, 5, 4
♡ 4   N   ♡ Q, 10, 8, 7, 6
◇ A, Q, 10, 8, 7 W   E   ◇ 6, 5
♣ Q, 9, 7, 5, 3   S   ♣ 10, 2

        ♠ A, J, 3
        ♡ A, K, 5, 2
        ◇ J, 9, 4
        ♣ A, J, 4

West led the queen of diamonds and declarer covered with the king from dummy, which held the trick. He continued with the queen of spades, ducked by East, and another spade to the jack. Disappointingly, the ace failed to drop the king. Keeping in reserve the club finesse, declarer now played the ace and king of hearts, hoping to drop the queen. However, when West showed void on the second round, Mr Parker considered the hand again. West was known to have started with ten cards in the minors and, as East had followed to the first diamond, he could not have held more than six in that suit. If West had held only five diamonds then declarer could safely throw him in with a diamond to lead up to the clubs. But a slightly better plan occurred to him. He cashed the ace and king of clubs, in case East held Q, x and then threw West in with the queen of clubs to lead up to his ◇ J, 9 from ◇ A, 10. This line of play loses only when East holds precisely ♣ Q, x, x.

Isidor Kerman, the well-known lawyer, only plays rubber bridge. But besides being a skilful skier, he is a natural card-player who uses his common sense, and above all a most congenial partner. We meet every year in St Moritz at the rubber-bridge table.

The spirit of the rubber-bridge game at the Palace Hotel or at Suvretta House is mostly light-hearted; it is also influenced by the effect of the altitude on our mental and physical condition. All this will help to explain the bidding of the hand below. South dealt at game all and 60 to North–South and passed. West opened 1◇ and I did not like to pass (I very rarely do). I bid 1♡, East doubled and my partner, who would hardly remove the double unless he had a good reason, bid 1♠. West now bid 2♣ and East, who was convinced that I had psyched, jumped to 4♡. When this came round to me I doubled and East now committed one of his rare mistakes: he redoubled. I knew him as a solid player, so I began to review the defensive values of my hand. I came to the conclusion that East, who obviously held seven hearts, would probably make ten or eleven tricks. Anyhow it was obvious that my partner held a long suit of spades, so I decided to bid 4♠, which East (whose greed had led him to redouble 4♡) decided to double. Here are the four hands:

Markus
♠ A, 6
♡ 10, 9, 8, 7
♢ Q, 9, 8
♣ A, Q, 8, 4

♠ 5, 4, 2
♡ K
♢ A, K, 7, 6, 5
♣ K, 10, 9, 3

♠ Q, 7
♡ A, Q, J, 6, 5, 3, 2
♢ J, 10, 3, 2
♣ None

Kerman
♠ K, J, 10, 9, 8, 3
♡ 4
♢ 4
♣ J, 7, 6, 5, 2

West led the king of diamonds and then the king of hearts. East overtook this with the ace and played the 2 of hearts, obviously asking for a club.

But our friend Kerman was not to be fooled: he ruffed with the 10 of trumps and in so doing he located the queen of trumps. He then drew the trumps and played the jack of clubs. West covered and declarer took the trick with the ace. Next he played the 8 of clubs from dummy. West won this trick, but then could do nothing but play the ace of diamonds or a club into declarer's tenace. So we scored 790 and won the rubber. A more experienced East would have played the 2 of hearts on partner's king. West might then have switched to the 3 of clubs and beaten the contract, as he must still come to his club trick.

When the rubber-bridge-playing skiers have left and St Moritz enters its "quiet season" (January 15 – February 1) the bridge competitors move in to participate in Count Fabricotti's brainchild "The St Moritz Bridge Festival". Many of the famous arrive, but there are enough amateurs to turn this event into a jolly party. Every year I am invited to field a team from Britain. I usually play with Mrs Fritzi Gordon and on this occasion Michael Wolach and Louis Tarlo completed our team. Michael Wolach chose the following sequence of play on a hand in the team event where careful thought was needed to avoid possible bad breaks and doomed finesses. West dealt at love all:

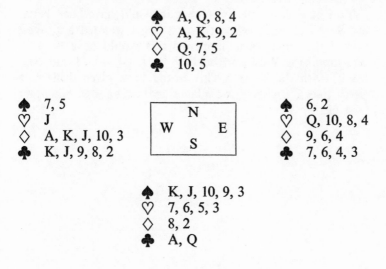

♠ A, Q, 8, 4
♡ A, K, 9, 2
◇ Q, 7, 5
♣ 10, 5

♠ 7, 5
♡ J
◇ A, K, J, 10, 3
♣ K, J, 9, 8, 2

N W E S

♠ 6, 2
♡ Q, 10, 8, 4
◇ 9, 6, 4
♣ 7, 6, 4, 3

♠ K, J, 10, 9, 3
♡ 7, 6, 5, 3
◇ 8, 2
♣ A, Q

West opened the bidding with 1◇, North doubled and after East had passed, South bid 2♠. North raised to 3♠ and South went on to game.

Against 4♠ West led the ace, king and another diamond. The temptation here was to discard the queen of clubs on the queen of diamonds and rely on the hearts breaking 3–2. Wolach was more careful; he discarded a heart. He was well aware that the club finesse was likely to be wrong as West had opened the bidding, and that the club queen could be discarded later on the fourth heart if all went well.

Trumps were drawn in two rounds and then South led a heart towards dummy. West played the jack and dummy won with the ace. Declarer returned to his own hand with a trump in order to lead another heart towards dummy.

11

Had West followed low the 9 would have been finessed to ensure three tricks in the suit, but when West showed out on the second round declarer was able to prove his foresight in retaining the queen of clubs. He went up with the king of hearts, cashed the ace of clubs and then threw West in with the queen. Having nothing left in his hand but clubs and diamonds, West now had to give declarer a ruff and discard for his tenth trick.

You may think, perhaps, that it would have been better for South to duck when the first heart was led and West played the jack. As it happened this would have worked, but supposing West had held $\heartsuit$ Q, J, 10, 4 and had continued with the lowest? This would have given declarer a nasty guess, and a good player avoids guesses whenever possible.

February
Tel Aviv

The Israeli Festival of Bridge comes as an exciting contrast after St Moritz. A world that seems to be all white and blue gives place to green and gold, and the leisurely luxury of the winter-sports arena becomes the gay, bustling activity of a new and energetic country.

The mood of the competitions is keenness, and there is always a "gallery" of enthusiastic youngsters watching and learning. They could certainly take a tip from the following hand played by our own Harold Franklin, who is aptly known throughout the international bridge scene as "The Chief Tournament Director". For players and spectators alike his competitions run as smoothly as a Jacklin putt across a perfect green. He is also, of course, a top international player, but he can rarely be persuaded to take time off to join a team. However, he agreed to play with me in an exhibition match in Israel. South dealt at love all:

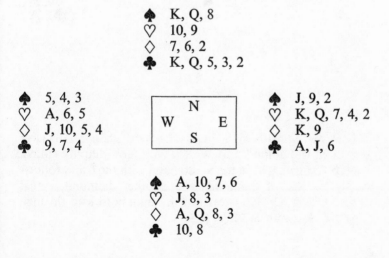

```
                ♠  K, Q, 8
                ♡  10, 9
                ◇  7, 6, 2
                ♣  K, Q, 5, 3, 2
♠  5, 4, 3          ┌──────────┐          ♠  J, 9, 2
♡  A, 6, 5          │    N     │          ♡  K, Q, 7, 4, 2
◇  J, 10, 5, 4     │ W     E  │          ◇  K, 9
♣  9, 7, 4          │    S     │          ♣  A, J, 6
                   └──────────┘
                ♠  A, 10, 7, 6
                ♡  J, 8, 3
                ◇  A, Q, 8, 3
                ♣  10, 8
```

13

After three passes East opened the bidding with 1♡ and a short battle of the suits left Harold, sitting South, as declarer in a dubious contract of 3♠.

West led the ace of hearts and switched to the 5 of spades. Dummy played the 8, East covered with the 9 and South won with the 10. He then led a club to dummy's queen, East refused to win with the ace, and declarer continued with a diamond finesse to his queen. Now another club was led from hand and ducked. East won with the jack, and realising that a trump return would enable the club suit to be set up, he smartly continued with ♡ K, Q to force dummy. Declarer, however, had other ideas; on the queen of hearts he discarded a diamond from dummy. This was now the position, with East to lead:

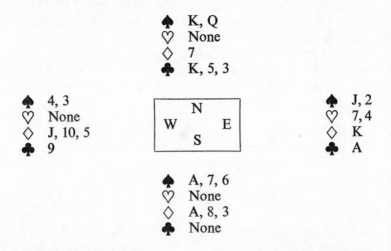

East continued with a heart – his best chance. Declarer discarded a diamond and West a club, and dummy ruffed. A club was trumped in the South hand with the 6 and followed by the ace of diamonds and another diamond, ruffed with the king. Declarer was now in dummy to lead through East's ♠ J, 2 into South's ♠ A, 7.

During the Israeli Bridge Festival of 1970 I played and won the pairs event with George Catzeflis, the Swiss international. He is one of my most charming partners and we have had several successes in a very short period. He is always alert to the many possibilities of most hands and it is an instruction in itself to watch him deftly weave his way through a poorish pairs-scoring contract towards a top. North dealt at game to North–South:

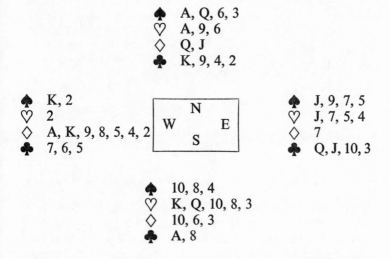

```
            ♠  A, Q, 6, 3
            ♡  A, 9, 6
            ◇  Q, J
            ♣  K, 9, 4, 2

♠ K, 2                          ♠ J, 9, 7, 5
♡ 2              N              ♡ J, 7, 5, 4
◇ A, K, 9, 8, 5, 4, 2  W   E    ◇ 7
♣ 7, 6, 5           S           ♣ Q, J, 10, 3

            ♠  10, 8, 4
            ♡  K, Q, 10, 8, 3
            ◇  10, 6, 3
            ♣  A, 8
```

I opened 1NT (strong) on the North hand, George bid 3♡ and West came in with 4◇. I raised to 4♡ and all passed.

West cashed the ace and king of diamonds and East discarded a spade. West continued with a diamond. My partner considered dummy carefully and realised that ten tricks in no-trumps would be easy if the spade finesse worked – which was likely on the bidding. So to change a bad score to a good one he had to aim at making 5♡. He ruffed the third diamond with the ace of trumps and East now discarded the 3 of clubs. Declarer then played the 9 of hearts and let it run. He continued with the trump suit and drew all the missing trumps, discarding two low spades from

15

dummy on the third and fourth rounds. At this stage he could, of course, have made his eleven tricks by ruffing out the clubs, but as yet he could not complete a count of the hands. He therefore finessed the spade, cashed the ace and returned to his own hand with the ace of clubs. East did his best to avoid the impending squeeze by playing the jack of clubs giving declarer a choice of plays, as you can see:

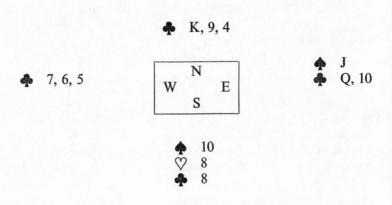

South now played his last trump, discarding the 4 of clubs from dummy, and East nonchalantly let go the queen of clubs. Declarer was not fooled – he knew by now that East had started life with a 4-4-1-4 distribution and therefore had another club as well as the jack of spades. But which club? There was no good reason why East should discard the queen, hold on to a low club and give declarer a free finesse position unless that finesse was going to lose! So he led his 8 of clubs towards dummy and firmly played the king, smiling quietly to himself when East's 10 duly dropped under it.

Louis Shenkin, chairman of the British Bridge League (BBL), goes every year to the Israeli Bridge Festival and he brings many of his jolly Scottish friends with him. I like him very much, but on this occasion, when he sat on my left and produced a "coup" which left me speechless, I was not so fond of him.

It is not easy to do well in Israel; it took me several years to convince my friends that I could win there. The hospitality and the wonderful sight-seeing possibilities have the effect that we get to the table too exhausted to count or to follow every trick with the necessary concentration. What would you do when the bidding has gone:

South	West	North	East
2♣	NB	7NT	NB
NB	?		

I made a big mistake. I doubled on ♠ J, 7, 3, 2; ♡ A, 9, 3; ♢ 8, 6, 4; ♣ 10, 9, 3. I knew that if Louis made 7NT we should have a bad result and hoped that my partner would guess and lead a heart! When you look at the hand you will find that there are two leads to beat the contract – the 6 of spades or a heart. My partner led a club, and look what happened to yours truly:

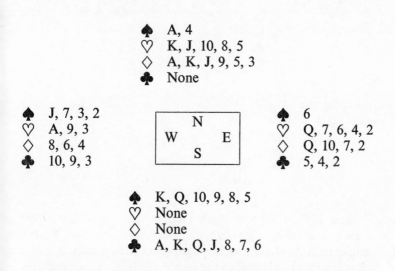

I had to find four discards on dummy's clubs and then declarer (North) played a low spade to the ace in his own hand

and cashed his two top diamonds. So I now had the enviable choice between discarding the ace of hearts and abandoning the guard in spades.

While waiting for the scores after a tournament session some players pass the time playing a few rubbers. On such an occasion Dr Fritz Chodziesner found a way to make a contract in a most unusual manner. His bid of 3♡ was well judged because of the score; North–South had a game and 30 below the line. South dealt:

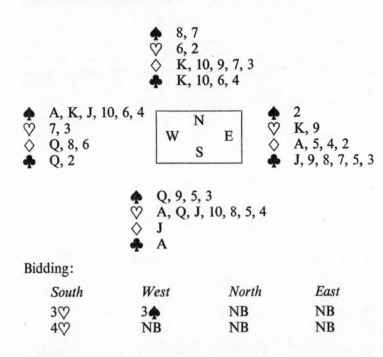

♠ 8, 7
♡ 6, 2
◇ K, 10, 9, 7, 3
♣ K, 10, 6, 4

♠ A, K, J, 10, 6, 4
♡ 7, 3
◇ Q, 8, 6
♣ Q, 2

N
W   E
S

♠ 2
♡ K, 9
◇ A, 5, 4, 2
♣ J, 9, 8, 7, 5, 3

♠ Q, 9, 5, 3
♡ A, Q, J, 10, 8, 5, 4
◇ J
♣ A

Bidding:

South	West	North	East
3♡	3♠	NB	NB
4♡	NB	NB	NB

West led the king of spades, declarer dropped the 9 and East's 2 confused his partner. He did not realise that it could be a singleton, so he interpreted it as a request for a club lead and switched to the queen of clubs. South took the trick, played the jack of diamonds and let it run to East's ace.

East did the best he could: he played the king of hearts! Dr Chodziesner eyed this "Greek gift" with suspicion. Winning the trick with the ace he played the 8 of trumps and East was again on lead.

This was the picture:

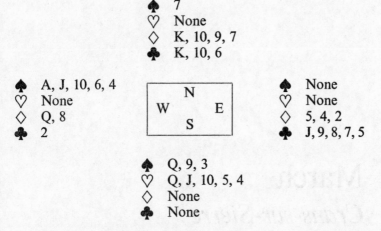

East had now to give dummy an entry and in so doing also had to "take" a finesse for declarer in one of the minor suits, thus providing three discards for South's losing spades. It was lucky for declarer to find East with the 9 of trumps, but not many players would have thought of this unusual solution to a problem which seemed impossible to solve.

March

Crans-sur-Sierre

The Swiss are rightly proud of their winter resorts, and Crans-sur-Sierre – a small, dream-like resort near the Italian border – has all the makings of a perfect holiday. It is primarily famous for its golf course, which is probably the nicest mountain course in Europe; but in the lengthening days of March its chief attractions are its excellent ski-runs, equipped with every facility for beginners, average performers and experts alike. Only when it gets dark does one hurry to the Golf Hotel, where Toni Trad is busy organising an exciting bridge week – an event which has grown apace in popularity and importance.

Here is an interesting hand from a recent Individual competition at Crans. Whatever the contract, tempo was what mattered. West dealt at love all:

♠ 10, 6, 5
♡ A, J, 6, 4
◇ 10, 6, 3
♣ 10, 7, 4

Mrs Y. Kutner

♠ K, 8, 3
♡ 7, 2
◇ 9, 8, 2
♣ K, Q, J, 9, 2

```
        N
    W       E
        S
```

♠ A, 7, 4
♡ 9, 3
◇ Q, J, 7, 5
♣ A, 8, 5, 3

♠ Q, J, 9, 2
♡ K, Q, 10, 8, 5
◇ A, K, 4
♣ 6

Bidding:

West	North	East	South
NB	NB	1♣	Double
3♣	NB	NB	3♡
NB	4♡	NB	NB
NB			

Against 4♡ East–West had to find an early diamond attack before the losing diamond disappeared on the long spade. Mrs Y. Kutner of Switzerland, the eventual winner, opened with the king of clubs and immediately switched to a diamond. When declarer tried to set up the spades, another diamond attack cleared the suit while her partner still had the ace of spades.

When the hand was played by East–West in clubs the defence had to tackle the spade early on to gain the tempo against declarer's diamond suit. South, of course, had been in the bidding, so it was easy to read him for ◇ A, K and chance a finesse against the 10.

21

My partner (whom I had just met for the first time), and I gained a fortunate top on this board. As we sat down I said, as I always do when partnering someone I haven't played with before, "I play natural bridge. Two Clubs, Strong No-Trump and Blackwood." Our opposition started a curious conversation in two different languages and eventually the gentleman pushed a sheet of closely written hieroglyphics across to his partner. She studied this hopelessly for a moment and then announced that she spoke only Italian. As the sheet was in French it was not of much help to her.

My partner, sitting East, opened 1◇ in third position, and after South had made a take-out double I bid 1NT. I didn't consider my hand suitable for a redouble and I like the semi-pre-emptive value of 1NT in this situation. The bidding was passed round to South, who now made the ambiguous bid of 2◇, which his partner mis-read and passed. I had no reason to mistrust my partner's opening bid so I kicked off with the 9 of diamonds. South tried to establish his spades but we were able to clear his other diamond honour, draw trumps and cash all our clubs for nine tricks. South could have salvaged one trick by engineering a club ruff in his own hand.

As I say again and again – keep it simple, especially when you sit down and play only two hands with a stranger. South could have doubled again instead of bidding 2◇, which if misunderstood could (as it did) lead to disaster. It would not have mattered what interpretation his partner put on a second double. A diamond or heart lead would have ensured the defeat of 1NT if the double were treated as "for penalties", and if not, the natural bid of 2♡ would have resulted in the correct contract.

I have told this story before and I expect I shall tell it again despite the fact that it goes against me. Come sit behind me, dear reader, and play this hand. Try and share the agonies I suffered.

The bidding has been short and uninformative; sitting South I have opened 1NT and my partner has raised to 3NT.

♠ Q, 8, 7
♡ Q, 9, 8, 7
◇ A, 10, 6
♣ K, 5, 3

```
      N
  W       E
      S
```

♠ A, 5, 4
♡ K, 6
◇ K, 8, 7, 2
♣ A, J, 10, 4

West leads the jack of hearts; 7 from dummy, 2 from East, and I win with the king. I shoot back my 6 of hearts; 3 from West and dummy's 8 holds the trick, East following with the 4. The club finesse, I think, don't you? To protect my entries I lead low from dummy towards the 10, East playing the 6, but West wins with the queen and continues with the 2. I win with the king in dummy and cash another club to see how they fall. Both opponents follow, so let's have a recap.

West has evidently started life with ♡ A, J, 10, 5, 3 and ♣ Q, x, x, leaving him with five cards in spades and diamonds. I would like to cash another club but I am not sure what I can safely throw from dummy yet. West may have the king of spades as he didn't open the suit when in with the queen of clubs. We'll bear that in mind.

The diamond suit seems the best bet now. I lead a diamond from hand, West plays the 5, I insert the 10 from dummy and East wins with the jack. He continues with the 3 of diamonds, I play the 7, West the 9 and dummy wins the ace. Now another diamond; East contributes the 4. . . . We know that East has only spades and diamonds left and that West is short in diamonds so I think I should try the finesse here.

23

Even if West does win the queen, he will have to give me a heart trick or lead from his very likely king of spades. So we finesse the diamond and West wins with his queen. He follows with a low spade, happily I go up with the queen, happily East plays the king, and unhappily I go one down.

Now *you* explain to my partner why ours was the solitary minus score on the sheet. All the other Souths had made 600, 630 or even 660. Here are the four hands:

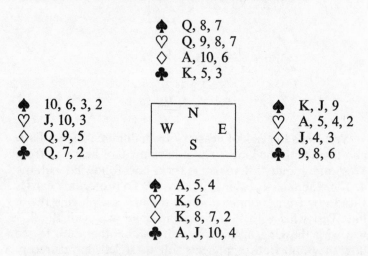

♠ Q, 8, 7
♡ Q, 9, 8, 7
◇ A, 10, 6
♣ K, 5, 3

♠ 10, 6, 3, 2
♡ J, 10, 3
◇ Q, 9, 5
♣ Q, 7, 2

♠ K, J, 9
♡ A, 5, 4, 2
◇ J, 4, 3
♣ 9, 8, 6

♠ A, 5, 4
♡ K, 6
◇ K, 8, 7, 2
♣ A, J, 10, 4

I swear that East followed to the first and second heart tricks with his 2 and 4 without a flicker of emotion. I found later that most declarers had had a low spade led, and in an effort to keep the lead from West had finessed the club the abnormal way, against West, and then ducked the diamond to East for the same reason. (The only way to catch four clubs to the queen is to finesse against East.) The overtricks came when the defenders were careless in their discards on the long diamond and club, and declarer was able to engineer an end-play on East.

I watched sadly, dear reader, as I saw my partner touting the hand round, asking "How can a player like Rixi Markus go down in 3NT on this deal?" Ah well, perhaps he won't be playing in the Crans-sur-Sierre Individual next year – or perhaps I shall play under an assumed name!

In 1970 Mrs Gordon and I, with Toni Trad and Bernasconi as our complementary pair, won the team event at Crans-sur-Sierre. And here is a hand wonderfully played by Toni Trad of Switzerland which helped towards our victory. South dealt at game all:

```
                    ♠ Q, 3
                    ♡ A, 9, 4
                    ◇ J, 10, 6, 3
                    ♣ Q, J, 7, 2

♠ None                  N           ♠ J, 9, 5, 4, 2
♡ Q, 10, 8, 7, 6    W       E       ♡ K, J, 5, 2
◇ K, 5, 4, 2            S            ◇ 7
♣ 10, 9, 8, 4                       ♣ 6, 5, 3

                    ♠ A, K, 10, 8, 7, 6
                    ♡ 3
                    ◇ A, Q, 9, 8
                    ♣ A, K
```

Bidding:

South	West	North	East
2♣	NB	2♡[1]	NB
2♠	NB	3♠	NB
4◇[2]	NB	5◇	NB
6♠	NB	NB	NB

[1] Showing the ace.
[2] A cue bid.

The contract was a perfectly normal one, but as the cards lay it required great skill to fulfil it.

West led the 10 of clubs and Toni won in hand. He tested the trumps by leading towards his queen in dummy, and when West showed void he went into a huddle. On the face of it the contract would seem to depend on the diamond finesse coming off. But Toni, like most expert players, likes to avoid finesses whenever there is another way, and he found a perfect solution. He led another trump from dummy, finessed the 7 (this, of course, was a "marked" finesse) and cashed the ace of trumps. The ace of clubs followed by the ace of diamonds came next, and then declarer crossed to dummy with the ace of hearts and cashed the queen of clubs, discarding a diamond. This was now the position:

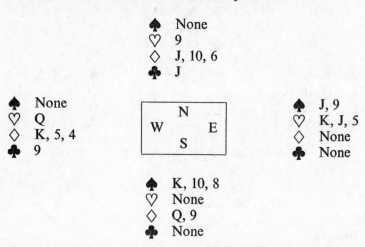

♠ None
♡ 9
◇ J, 10, 6
♣ J

♠ None
♡ Q
◇ K, 5, 4
♣ 9

N
W   E
S

♠ J, 9
♡ K, J, 5
◇ None
♣ None

♠ K, 10, 8
♡ None
◇ Q, 9
♣ None

Now the jack of clubs from North; if East ruffs South overruffs, draws the last trump and gives up a diamond; so East discarded and South let go another diamond. He led a heart from dummy, which he ruffed, and his hand now consisted only of ♠ K, 10 and ◇Q. When he led his queen of diamonds West had to win and lead another diamond through East's J, 9 of trumps. You will see the essential point of cashing the ace of diamonds before East has time to discard his singleton. The beauty of this play is that it cannot lose, for if East has the king of diamonds he has to lead into South's spade tenace eventually and the same result is obtained.

April
Cannes

You may approve or disapprove of Casinos and gambling, but many bridge events could not take place without the generous support of the French Casinos – especially those under the efficient management of M. Barrière at Cannes, Deauville, Juan-les-Pins and La Baule.

The Spring Festival at Cannes is a glittering fixture in the bridge calendar. The players all enjoy the luxuries of the five-star Hotel Majestic, the tournament is held at the Casino, and as an added attraction you can watch an exhibition match every evening between the greatest stars of Italy and the best French experts. So far Italy has won on each occasion – but who can tell, after the brilliant French victory in Estoril (October 1970), what the future holds? Here is a hand beautifully executed by Gerard Desrousseaux (according to some, the best technician in the French camp). His partner, sitting North, opened 1NT (vulnerable), the non-vulnerable East came in with 2♠, Desrousseaux doubled, West bid 3♡, North passed, East passed, South bid 3♠ and North raised to 4♠, which was doubled by East. Here are the four hands:

```
                    ♠  K, 7
                    ♡  A, Q
                    ◇  K, Q, 9, 7
                    ♣  Q, J, 6, 5, 4

♠  None                    N              ♠  A, J, 10, 3, 2
♡  K, J, 10, 8, 6, 4, 2             W  E  ♡  5
◇  J, 4, 2          W           E         ◇  A, 10, 8, 6, 5
♣  9, 8, 7                 S              ♣  K, 2

                    ♠  Q, 9, 8, 6, 5, 4
                    ♡  9, 7, 3
                    ◇  3
                    ♣  A, 10, 3
```

West led the 9 of clubs, which would have been a good lead if the no-trump bidder had held the ace. East allowed dummy's jack to hold the trick and declarer now had to do some hard thinking. East was marked with all the missing trumps. Declarer could not afford to lose more than two trump tricks as he was bound to lose one trick in diamonds. He eventually decided on the following plan: he played the 7 of spades from dummy.

Try your skill at defending and you will soon have to admit that there is now no way of beating the contract. In fact East played low and the 7 held the trick. Declarer next led a club towards his ace and played a diamond, and the queen was taken by East's ace. East cashed the ace of spades and played his singleton heart, and here is the full picture at this stage:

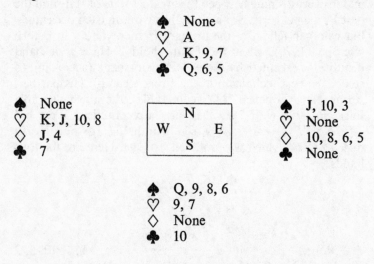

```
                    ♠ None
                    ♡ A
                    ◇ K, 9, 7
                    ♣ Q, 6, 5

♠ None                              ♠ J, 10, 3
♡ K, J, 10, 8         N             ♡ None
◇ J, 4          W         E         ◇ 10, 8, 6, 5
♣ 7                  S             ♣ None

                    ♠ Q, 9, 8, 6
                    ♡ 9, 7
                    ◇ None
                    ♣ 10
```

Having won the heart trick in dummy, declarer discarded the 10 of clubs on the king of diamonds and then continued to play clubs. East was in a hopeless position. He refused to ruff, so declarer discarded his two hearts and then ruffed a diamond. Had East ruffed, declarer would have over-ruffed; he was then long enough in trumps to draw the remaining trumps and enter dummy with the ace of hearts.

This is a fascinating hand because, although declarer lacks safe entries in dummy, he can still achieve ten tricks by a correct reading of East's holding. It is an excellent exercise for any inquisitive bridge mind. Try and make the contract on a heart lead (the most unfavourable lead for declarer), or try and defeat it. Careful planning by declarer should beat the best defence.

Here is a hand played by the late Dr Theron (who was one of the best-liked figures in international bridge), with all the panache we have come to expect at the Cannes Festival. North dealt at game to North–South:

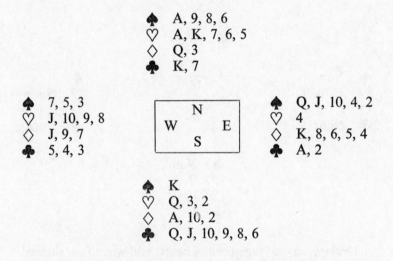

```
                    ♠ A, 9, 8, 6
                    ♡ A, K, 7, 6, 5
                    ◇ Q, 3
                    ♣ K, 7

  ♠ 7, 5, 3           ┌─────────┐     ♠ Q, J, 10, 4, 2
  ♡ J, 10, 9, 8       │    N    │     ♡ 4
  ◇ J, 9, 7           │ W     E │     ◇ K, 8, 6, 5, 4
  ♣ 5, 4, 3           │    S    │     ♣ A, 2
                      └─────────┘
                    ♠ K
                    ♡ Q, 3, 2
                    ◇ A, 10, 2
                    ♣ Q, J, 10, 9, 8, 6
```

North opened the bidding with 1♡ and East found a typical match-point double, but North–South ignored his interference and reached 6♣.

West led the 7 of spades, won by the king. Theron could see that if the hearts broke 3–2 there was no problem, but he would not have sufficient entries to ruff the fourth heart and enjoy the fifth. He led a trump to the king. East won and continued with a spade, won in dummy, declarer discarding the 2 of diamonds. Then declarer cleared the trumps. It seemed from East's double that he must hold the king of diamonds, but where was the jack? Theron decided to assume that the missing diamond honours were split, and on this basis to try for the elegant transfer-menace squeeze: he could then leave the heart suit intact to fall back on if all else failed. He therefore played off all his trumps but one, crossed to the ace of hearts and led the queen of diamonds, which was covered by East and won with the ace in hand, leaving this position:

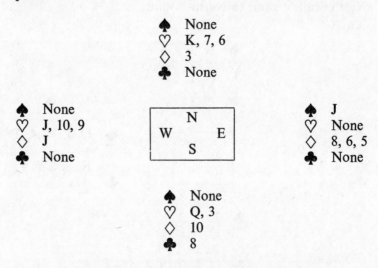

```
                        ♠  None
                        ♡  K, 7, 6
                        ◇  3
                        ♣  None

    ♠  None                  ┌──────────┐        ♠  J
    ♡  J, 10, 9              │    N     │        ♡  None
    ◇  J                     │ W     E  │        ◇  8, 6, 5
    ♣  None                  │    S     │        ♣  None
                             └──────────┘

                        ♠  None
                        ♡  Q, 3
                        ◇  10
                        ♣  8
```

Declarer cashed the queen of hearts and when East showed out he was thankful for his foresight. West was in trouble now when South played his last trump: he had either to part with the jack of diamonds, promoting South's 10 to a winner, or to discard his heart guard.

Coincidence has a long arm, I know, but I found out at Cannes that it can be a two-handed arm. Take these two hands:

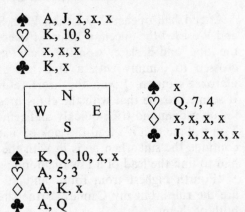

```
                ♠  A, J, x, x, x
                ♡  K, 10, 8
                ◇  x, x, x
                ♣  K, x
♠  x, x                              ♠  x
♡  J, 9, 6, 2      ┌─────────┐      ♡  Q, 7, 4
◇  Q, J, 10        │    N    │      ◇  x, x, x, x
♣  10, x, x, x     │ W     E │      ♣  J, x, x, x, x
                   │    S    │
                   └─────────┘
                ♠  K, Q, 10, x, x
                ♡  A, 5, 3
                ◇  A, K, x
                ♣  A, Q
```

South played in 6♠ and Mrs Gordon (West) led the queen
of diamonds. Declarer won, drew trumps, cashed his clubs
and threw West in with the third diamond. He was, of course,
hoping that West would have to make a damaging heart
lead or give him a ruff and discard. But my partner was wide
awake and found the only card to break the contract. She
returned the jack of hearts. Declarer had no answer to this.

I am very ambitious about defence. With a good partner
you can try and beat contracts which seem unbeatable;
but you need co-operation, which you only get from a first-
class player. Here it was Benito Garozzo who understood my
reason for an unorthodox but successful attempt to beat
4♠, which was made at every other table.

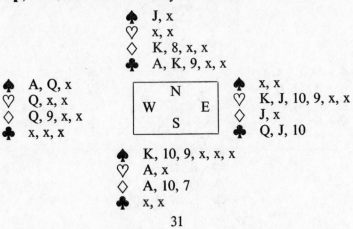

```
                ♠  J, x
                ♡  x, x
                ◇  K, 8, x, x
                ♣  A, K, 9, x, x
♠  A, Q, x                           ♠  x, x
♡  Q, x, x         ┌─────────┐      ♡  K, J, 10, 9, x, x
◇  Q, 9, x, x      │    N    │      ◇  J, x
♣  x, x, x         │ W     E │      ♣  Q, J, 10
                   │    S    │
                   └─────────┘
                ♠  K, 10, 9, x, x, x
                ♡  A, x
                ◇  A, 10, 7
                ♣  x, x
```

After I had opened 3♡ sitting East, South played in 4♠ and West led the queen of hearts. I overtook the queen with the king, and declarer won the trick with the ace. He then crossed to dummy with a club and finessed a spade to Garozzo's queen. I won the heart return, but what now? It seemed to me that with the clubs breaking even I had to set up a diamond trick quickly and remove dummy's entry. You will see that if I lead the jack of diamonds West cannot continue the suit when he is in with the ace of spades, so I had to find the lead of a low diamond.

"Fourth highest from four" and "top of a doubleton" are the rules, but my Cannes partnerships needed to break both of them.

I enjoy playing with Leon Tintner. Like me he is of Viennese origin, and he shares many of my ideas. He has played for a long time in the strongest French bridge group. He has won European and many other titles and we have had numerous successes together. Here is a hand from the mixed pairs in Cannes, which we managed to win in front of Forquet and Catherine Stoppa.

In fourth position I decided to open 2♣. My partner bid 2◊, I bid 2NT and he gave me 3NT. West was on lead and although I felt sorry for him, I enjoyed this hand very much:

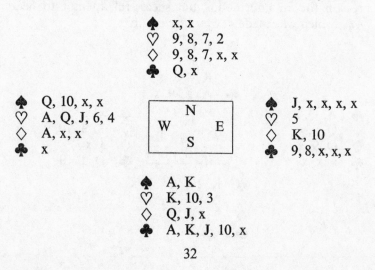

♠ x, x
♡ 9, 8, 7, 2
◊ 9, 8, 7, x, x
♣ Q, x

♠ Q, 10, x, x
♡ A, Q, J, 6, 4
◊ A, x, x
♣ x

♠ J, x, x, x, x
♡ 5
◊ K, 10
♣ 9, 8, x, x, x

♠ A, K
♡ K, 10, 3
◊ Q, J, x
♣ A, K, J, 10, x

32

West led the ace of hearts – can you blame him? I did not hesitate but played the 10. He then played a low heart and I was in dummy with the 7. I now led a diamond from dummy and East played the king, which held the trick. East then played a spade. I conceded one more diamond for ten tricks and a very good result.

May
Juan-les-Pins

Juan-les-Pins is, of course, one of the most popular of the French summer-holiday resorts; fortunately its bridge festival usually takes place in May, just as the wonderful weather starts. Situated between Cannes and Nice, within striking distance of Monte Carlo, and with the breath-taking scenery of the Alps for car trips, it offers a memorable holiday for the whole family. I have friends who own a villa hugging the mountainside, with a panoramic view of the Mediterranean, and I often stay there for a few days after the bridge festival is over, accompanying my hosts to the exciting Monaco Grand Prix motor race.

The bridge festival is one of the oldest of its kind: 1971 was its 22nd year. I have seldom missed it, and I still cannot find words to describe the charm of this jewel among the resorts of the French Riviera. Most British players choose to stay at the lovely Hotel Provençal, with its two beaches and excellent cuisine – probably the best food I have ever tasted in a beach restaurant.

The bridge events take place in the Palm Beach Casino overlooking the sea. The programme is so arranged that one can spend the day on the beaches or sight-seeing before starting to play at about four o'clock. The session ends around eight o'clock in plenty of time to change for the late evening meal and enjoy the soft warm air with the delicate

scent of the famous pines as one strolls to the Casino for a
flutter at the tables.

Under the direction of the famous tournament director,
I. Bajos de Heredia, and the management of the indefatigable
Monsieur Leyrat, the competitions get smoothly, if a little
boisterously, under way.

Smooth was the word for Joe Amesbury's play as South
on this hand, and boisterous was the post-mortem by the
opposition. South dealt at love all:

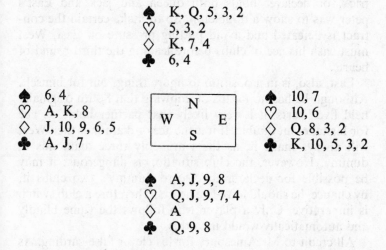

♠ K, Q, 5, 3, 2
♡ 5, 3, 2
◇ K, 7, 4
♣ 6, 4

♠ 6, 4
♡ A, K, 8
◇ J, 10, 9, 6, 5
♣ A, J, 7

N
W   E
S

♠ 10, 7
♡ 10, 6
◇ Q, 8, 3, 2
♣ K, 10, 5, 3, 2

♠ A, J, 9, 8
♡ Q, J, 9, 7, 4
◇ A
♣ Q, 9, 8

South opened the bidding with 1♠, West doubled and North,
I. Baron Egmont von Dewitz, pre-empted to 4♠, which
became the final contract.

West led the king of hearts, East played the 10 and South
the 7. West continued with the ace and 8 of hearts, East
ruffing the third round and declarer following with the 9 and
jack. East now switched to a diamond, and declarer was able
to draw trumps and discard dummy's two losing clubs on his
two winning hearts.

"I thought your 8 of hearts was your highest – the 4 was still missing – and meant you wanted a diamond," said East.

"It was the only heart I had left," replied West shortly.

But he, too, could have prevented this debacle with a little thought. When his partner commenced a peter in hearts it was clear that he must hold either the queen or a doubleton. He could not hold both queen and jack, or he would have played the queen instead of the 10 on the opening lead. Therefore it should be apparent to West that either declarer holds the jack of hearts and East's queen will win the third trick, or declarer holds both queen and jack and East's peter was to show a doubleton. So to make certain the contract is defeated and avoid putting pressure on East, West must cash his ace of clubs before leading the third round of hearts.

East, also, is in a position to figure things out for himself. Although he has no means of knowing that South originally held five hearts, it is very likely that partner holds an ace for his take-out double. If it is the ace of diamonds then West will always make it, as there are only three diamonds in dummy. However, the club situation is dangerous: it may be possible for declarer to discard dummy's two clubs if, by chance, he should have five hearts. Therefore a club switch is imperative. Only a player who follows the game blindly and automatically would miss this.

All credit to Mr Amesbury for his clever false-carding. As he said, "When East played the 10 of hearts I wasn't sure quite what was afoot, but I dropped the 7 to leave myself manoeuvring space. When West continued with the ace and East completed the peter I had, somehow, to try and persuade him not to switch to a club when he obtained his ruff, so I concealed the 4. It worked, thank goodness."

But it shouldn't have worked. Even with all the gadgets we employ these days there are still hands where we have to use our native "savvy". Much confusion is caused by attempts to read a special meaning into every card played by partner.

Inexperienced players are often afraid of playing contracts with only a 4–3 fit in the trump suit. It is true that such contracts are difficult, particularly when the suit is not solid, but sometimes there is no other choice. As a rule it is safer in these circumstances not to touch trumps immediately in case the opposition's holding is unevenly divided. Here is a hand where my partner, Mrs Fritzi Gordon, deftly threaded her way across the quicksands of distribution. South dealt at love all:

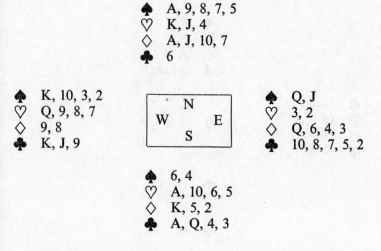

```
                 ♠ A, 9, 8, 7, 5
                 ♡ K, J, 4
                 ◇ A, J, 10, 7
                 ♣ 6

♠ K, 10, 3, 2           N           ♠ Q, J
♡ Q, 9, 8, 7       W         E      ♡ 3, 2
◇ 9, 8                  S           ◇ Q, 6, 4, 3
♣ K, J, 9                           ♣ 10, 8, 7, 5, 2

                 ♠ 6, 4
                 ♡ A, 10, 6, 5
                 ◇ K, 5, 2
                 ♣ A, Q, 4, 3
```

The Bidding:

South	West	North	East
1♡	NB	1♠	NB
1NT	NB	3◇	NB
3NT	NB	4♡	NB
NB	NB		

I considered leaving my partner in 3NT, but this was a pairs competition and I thought my ruffing value might provide extra tricks. In fact 3NT is likely to go down on a spade lead.

Against 4♡ West led the 9 of diamonds. Declarer played the 10 from dummy and East played low. Mrs Gordon immediately led a low spade from dummy, East's jack winning the trick. A club was led and declarer won with the ace. She followed with the king of diamonds and a club ruff, then ace and a low spade, East discarding a club and declarer ruffing. She now ruffed another club in dummy with the jack and another spade in hand. This was the resulting position, with South to lead:

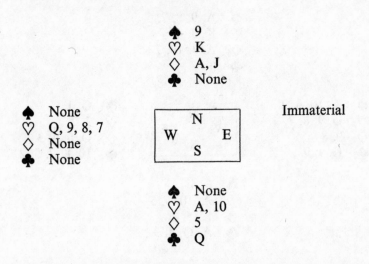

	♠ 9	
	♡ K	
	◇ A, J	
	♣ None	
♠ None		Immaterial
♡ Q, 9, 8, 7		
◇ None		
♣ None		
	♠ None	
	♡ A, 10	
	◇ 5	
	♣ Q	

Declarer led her last club; West had, perforce, to ruff: and dummy overruffed with the king. When dummy now played the ace of diamonds West had to trump and lead into declarer's ♡ A, 10. Thus declarer made eleven tricks in a contract which many players would not even know how to begin to play.

By contrast here is a defence, played by the famous French internationals Tintner and Deruy, which went with the smoothness of a billiard ball cannoning from cushion to cushion. East dealt with North–South vulnerable:

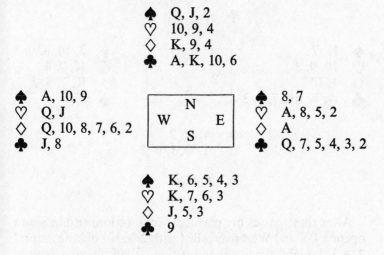

♠ Q, J, 2
♡ 10, 9, 4
◇ K, 9, 4
♣ A, K, 10, 6

♠ A, 10, 9
♡ Q, J
◇ Q, 10, 8, 7, 6, 2
♣ J, 8

♠ 8, 7
♡ A, 8, 5, 2
◇ A
♣ Q, 7, 5, 4, 3, 2

♠ K, 6, 5, 4, 3
♡ K, 7, 6, 3
◇ J, 5, 3
♣ 9

After three passes North opened the bidding with 1♣, South responded 1♠ and West intervened with 2◇. North raised to 2♠ and all passed.

Tintner, sitting West, led the 7 of diamonds, declarer played low in dummy and East (Deruy) won with the ace and returned the 8 of hearts. As yet declarer knew very little about the hand, and he played low. West won with the queen and returned a diamond, which East ruffed, following with the ace and another heart. West trumped, gave East another diamond ruff and sat back to wait for his ace of trumps to take the seventh defensive trick.

At the beginning of the third session of a pairs event at Juan-les-Pins my partner and I were not doing too well, so I was looking for a "swing" hand when this one came along. West dealt at game to East–West:

```
                    ♠  9, 5, 4
                    ♡  5, 3
                    ◇  A, Q, 9, 8, 3
                    ♣  Q, 8, 4

♠  K, 7                                        ♠  J, 10, 8, 6, 3
♡  10, 9, 8            ┌─────────────┐         ♡  K, 7, 4
◇  J, 10              │      N      │         ◇  K, 7, 5, 2
♣  A, K, 10, 7, 5, 3 │  W       E  │         ♣  6
                      │      S      │
                      └─────────────┘
                    ♠  A, Q, 2
                    ♡  A, Q, J, 6, 2
                    ◇  6, 4
                    ♣  J, 9, 2
```

After three passes my partner (Mrs Gordon) sitting South opened 1♡ and West overcalled with 2♣. If I bid the natural 2◇, I thought, the likelihood is that I shall play the hand in that contract for a poorish score. No-trumps with the doubtful club guard and only 8 points is out, which leaves a pass or double. Ah, a double, that's a better idea. If they go one down doubled and vulnerable for 200 the score will be better than any part-score we can make, and if they go two down the resulting 500 points will be better than a non-vulnerable game for us. If they make it we shall achieve a bottom instead of a poor result – not so much in it unless you are doing well. And, of course, I can trust Mrs Gordon to remove the double if she doesn't like it.

So I doubled, all passed, and this was the surprising outcome.

I led the 5 of hearts, South won with the jack and returned a diamond to my ace. I continued hearts, South won the queen and cashed the ace, on which I discarded my lowest spade. Mrs Gordon could deduce from this that I held exactly three small spades and that there was no hurry to cash her ace before continuing with another heart. Declarer discarded a spade and I ruffed with the 8 of clubs. I put South in again with her ace of spades and she carried on the good work with yet another heart, which West ruffed with the 7 and I overruffed with my queen. Declarer ruffed the spade continuation and, placing me with four trumps for my double, attempted to draw all those outstanding. So my partner also made a trump trick and we scored 800 points. As you can see, we could have made 3NT owing to the lucky distribution, but this was infinitely more rewarding.

One of the leading pairs sitting East–West had a disaster too. After West had opened the bidding with 1♣ East responded 1♠ and South overcalled with 2♡ which was doubled by East. West made the fatal mistake of leading a top club and then switching to the king of spades; the defence was thrown out of gear and South ended up with ten tricks. It is a point to remember that when a player makes an overcall in this situation he is often expecting and hoping for a lead in the suit bid by his right-hand opponent.

Defence seems to be the better part of attack again on this hand, also from the pairs event at Juan-les-Pins. West dealt and East–West were vulnerable:

	♠	10, 8, 6, 4, 2
	♡	K, J, 10, 8
	◊	9, 5
	♣	10, 6

♠ K, 7, 3		♠ A, Q, J, 9, 5
♡ Q, 6, 5, 3	N	♡ A, 9
◊ 7, 2	W E	◊ K, 8
♣ A, 9, 7, 3	S	♣ K, J, 5, 2

	♠	None
	♡	7, 4, 2
	◊	A, Q, J, 10, 6, 4, 3
	♣	Q, 8, 4

After West and North had passed, Boris Schapiro, sitting East, opened the bidding with 1♠ and South called 4♦. This was passed round to East, who doubled. West, Jonathan Cansino, showed good judgment in not bidding 4♠ and passed.

The king of spades was led against 4♦ doubled. Declarer ruffed and played a low heart, finessing the 10. East had to think fast where his four tricks were coming from. Unless partner held the right honour in clubs or a diamond trick, he could not expect to defeat the contract. He played the 9 of hearts on dummy's 10 with no sign of emotion. Declarer successfully finessed in diamonds, and after several rounds of trumps he finessed a second round of hearts to East's ace. East now had a count of declarer's hand because his partner had played high–low in hearts, thus indicating four cards in that suit. His only chance was to pin the 10 of clubs in dummy by playing the king and then the jack, relying on his partner to hold both ace and 9 in that suit. In this way three club tricks could be made before declarer had a chance to discard a club on the long heart.

When Terence Reese and Bob Sheehan played this hand sitting North–South the bidding was the same until West's final bid: this time West decided to bid 4♠, which North doubled. South found the good lead of the 4 of hearts. Declarer played the queen from dummy, North covered with the king and declarer won with the ace. He led a trump to dummy's king and, when he discovered the bad news, he led a low club and finessed the jack. South won with the queen and continued with the 7 of hearts. North won and returned a diamond. South cashed his two diamond tricks and exited with a heart. Declarer could now come to only five trump tricks, one club trick and one heart trick for minus 800.

And here is a hand where Mrs Gordon and I made no mistake in the defence but declarer missed the point of the play, so we were lucky. South dealt at love all:

```
              ♠ A, 7, 4
              ♡ None
              ◇ 8, 6, 5, 4, 3
              ♣ A, Q, 9, 4, 2

♠ 3                    N           ♠ Q, 8
♡ K, Q, J, 6, 5, 4, 3      W   E   ♡ 10, 9, 8, 7, 2
◇ K, Q, J              S           ◇ 9, 7, 2
♣ 7, 6                             ♣ K, J, 10

              ♠ K, J, 10, 9, 6, 5, 2
              ♡ A
              ◇ A, 10
              ♣ 8, 5, 3
```

South opened the bidding with 1♠ and my partner, Mrs Gordon, sitting West, bid 4♡. North raised to 4♠ and I pushed on with 5♡. South bid 5♠ and all passed. Mrs Gordon led the king of diamonds. Declarer won, drew trumps in two rounds, and then finessed the 9 of clubs to my 10. Not wanting to give the game away about the diamond situation, and hoping my partner might have the ace of hearts and be able to remove dummy's last trump, I returned a heart. Declarer won with the ace and finessed another club to me, and we quickly cashed our diamond winner to get her one off.

Except in the unlikely event that West has led a singleton king of diamonds and declarer misguesses the club situation in the later play, the hand is a lay-down for five and in most cases will make six.

Suppose that after drawing trumps declarer cashes the ace of hearts and gets off play with a diamond. The North-South hands will now be:

43

♠ 7
♡ None
◇ 8, 6, 5
♣ A, Q, 9, 4

♠ J, 10, 9, 6, 5
♡ None
◇ None
♣ 8, 5, 3

If the hand that wins the diamond returns a heart, the eleventh trick comes from a ruff and discard, and declarer can make six if the diamonds break 3–3 or the club finesse succeeds. If West wins and continues with diamonds, the suit can now be established unless East shows void; in which case the end-play against East in clubs is marked. If West switches to a club, declarer ducks the lead to East, who can only return a diamond. Thus if the diamonds are no worse than 4–2 the eleventh trick can once again be established, for dummy holds entries in the 7 of trumps and the ace of clubs.

This is a typical example of what can be gained by making use of dummy's long suit, especially when it has been led and one loser in it is already unavoidable. There is plenty of time for a club finesse if everything else fails.

Mrs Gordon and I have not been lucky in our attempts to win the pairs event at Juan-les-Pins. But in the team events we have an excellent record, and we have both had several successes in the mixed pairs with different partners. We usually choose our second pair on the spot and Leon Tintner likes joining our team. He, like myself, loves to play with many different partners. In 1970 he played with Petersell and there was a funny incident at the final stage. We were playing our last match against one of the weakest teams in the field and we had to score 80 per cent to beat the leaders, one of the best French teams. Mrs Gordon and I had a fair session: there was one hand where we should have been in a beatable game contract, but by sheer luck we stopped at a part-score, and this looked like being a winning board. Two other boards were also good for us, and then came this beauty, dealt by West at game to East–West:

♠ x, x, x
♡ x
◇ J, x, x, x, x
♣ A, x, x, x

♠ A, 9, 8, x, x   ♠ K, x
♡ A, K, 8, 7   ♡ Q, J, 10, x, x
◇ K, 10, x, x   ◇ A, Q, x
♣ None   ♣ x, x, x

```
        N
    W       E
        S
```

♠ Q, J, 10
♡ 9, x, x
◇ x
♣ K, Q, J, 10, 9, 8

Bidding:

West	North	East	South
1♠	NB	2♡	3♣
3♡	4♣	4♡	5♣
6♡	7♣	Double	NB
7♡	NB	NB	Double[1]
NB	NB	NB	

[1] Having pushed them into 7♡ we had to double to save our honour.

Now comes the funny part of the story. Our other pair were not too far away and could not help hearing the last two bids: West bid 7♡ in a fairly loud voice and I doubled loudly because our opponents had mentioned that West was a bit deaf. A match consists of four boards only and we knew that our partners had already played this board. What we did not know was that they had allowed North–South to play in 7♣ doubled and considered 900 a meagre reward when they could have made 7♡ vulnerable. This upset them so much that when they doubled 3NT on the following board they got their wires crossed, so that instead of beating the contract for +300 they had allowed it to be made for +550. (This was the hand on which we had cleverly stopped in a part-score.)

Luckily for us, this is how East played her 7♡ doubled. After trumping the club lead in dummy she came to her own hand with the king of spades, on which I threw the queen in desperation. She then ruffed another club with a low trump in dummy, came to her own hand with the ace of diamonds to ruff another club, cashed the ace of hearts and then played another diamond – which I ruffed. So we scored +200. Our team-mates arrived with long faces, saying "We are very sorry, but we did not bid 7♡." "Never mind," said I, "we scored 200." "How?" "We doubled 7♡." "How could she go down?" "Would I double if I could not beat it?"

The leading French team looked enviously at our score, which gave us enough points to beat them at the post. It was a dramatic finish. This was an occasion when we had to be lucky indeed to win, and "Lady Luck" smiled on us.

Pre-emptive bids are a delicate subject, for their merits are sometimes arguable. Here is a hand where my justification was less than successful, but our complementary pair saved me from disgrace. East dealt with East–West vulnerable:

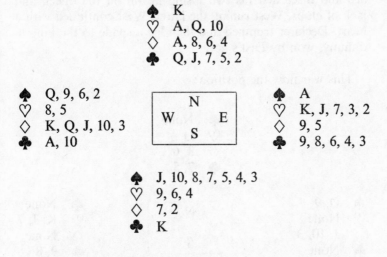

♠ K
♡ A, Q, 10
◇ A, 8, 6, 4
♣ Q, J, 7, 5, 2

♠ Q, 9, 6, 2
♡ 8, 5
◇ K, Q, J, 10, 3
♣ A, 10

♠ A
♡ K, J, 7, 3, 2
◇ 9, 5
♣ 9, 8, 6, 4, 3

♠ J, 10, 8, 7, 5, 4, 3
♡ 9, 6, 4
◇ 7, 2
♣ K

After East had passed I decided to put the cat among the pigeons and opened 3♠. West passed and my partner bid 4♠. When the bidding came round to West again he doubled happily and I realised that the cat had somehow got into our own aviary. I prepared my excuses for the lost 300 points while waiting for our other pair to join us to compare scores: "At this form of scoring, only four-board matches, we have to try for every game, and talk the opposition out of their games. After all, they can make 3NT or 4♡." My team-mates were not impressed.

"What did we lose on the board?" I asked.

"Oh, we didn't lose on the board, we gained; owing, of course, to our superior defence. They bid it the same way but we got them 500 down."

This was how it was done. West (Leon Tintner) led the king of diamonds. Declarer won with the ace in dummy and played a club, which was taken by West, who cashed his top diamond and switched to the 8 of hearts. Declarer went up with the ace and discarded his two losing hearts on the queen and jack of clubs, West ruffing the latter. West continued with a heart. Declarer trumped and then led a spade to the king in dummy, won by East's ace.

This was now the position:

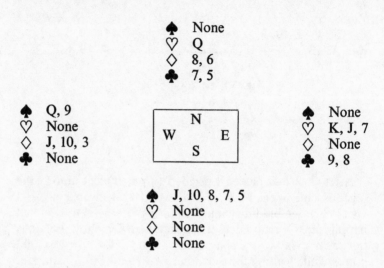

```
                      ♠  None
                      ♡  Q
                      ◇  8, 6
                      ♣  7, 5

♠  Q, 9            ┌─────────────┐        ♠  None
♡  None           │      N      │        ♡  K, J, 7
◇  J, 10, 3       │  W       E  │        ◇  None
♣  None           │      S      │        ♣  9, 8
                  └─────────────┘
                      ♠  J, 10, 8, 7, 5
                      ♡  None
                      ◇  None
                      ♣  None
```

East (Petersell) led a heart which South ruffed with the jack. Now West must come to two more trump tricks if he plays his cards right, but if he makes the mistake of overruffing he will make only his queen of trumps. He in fact discarded a diamond and was left with ♠ Q, 9 over South's 10, 8.

I have often written about Dr Chodziesner, the German international, and how extraordinary and newsworthy hands seem to gravitate towards him. Here is another one from the Juan-les-Pins festival which he played with great skill. West dealt with East–West vulnerable:

```
                      ♠  6, 4, 2
                      ♡  A, 6, 2
                      ◇  Q, 6, 2
                      ♣  K, 5, 3, 2
```

```
♠  Q, 10, 9, 3              ┌─────────────┐          ♠  A, J
♡  K, Q, 8, 7              │      N       │          ♡  J, 10, 9, 5, 3
◇  None                    │  W       E   │          ◇  K, 10, 9, 5
♣  J, 10, 8, 7, 6          │      S       │          ♣  A, 4
                          └─────────────┘
```

```
                      ♠  K, 8, 7, 5
                      ♡  4
                      ◇  A, J, 8, 7, 4, 3
                      ♣  Q, 9
```

The bidding:

West	North	East	South
NB	NB	1♡	2◇
4♡	5◇	Double	NB
NB	NB		

East–West did well to double 5◇ and not press on to
5♡, which could have been defeated. So now it was up to Dr
Chodziesner, sitting South, to make the non-vulnerable
sacrifice worth while.

West led the king of hearts. Declarer won with the ace
in dummy and played a spade. East took the trick with the
ace and continued with hearts, South ruffing. Declarer now
cashed the king of spades and played the queen of clubs.
East won with the ace and carried on with hearts, ruffed
again by declarer, and this was the position:

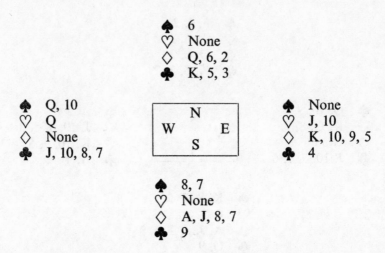

```
              ♠  6
              ♡  None
              ◇  Q, 6, 2
              ♣  K, 5, 3

♠  Q, 10              N              ♠  None
♡  Q            W        E           ♡  J, 10
◇  None              S              ◇  K, 10, 9, 5
♣  J, 10, 8, 7                      ♣  4

              ♠  8, 7
              ♡  None
              ◇  A, J, 8, 7
              ♣  9
```

Declarer now led a club to the king, and another club from dummy settled East's fate. In the event he discarded a heart. Declarer ruffed and continued with a spade, which was won by West, East discarding another heart. West played a club, which East ruffed with the 9 and declarer overruffed with the jack. A spade was trumped in dummy with the queen. East overruffed with his king but now had to lead from his 10, 5 into declarer's A, 8. Thus declarer lost only 300 points by sacrificing against 4♡ for East–West, which could not be beaten.

June
Monte Carlo

I don't think it is necessary to describe Monte Carlo; most of us have seen it in films or on the television news when the Monaco Grand Prix is on, even if we haven't been there. It still possesses a sort of fairy-tale atmosphere, with its pretty palace, its impressive casino and the white sails in the bay. There is something in the air which makes you feel romantic; so many dramas and happy events have taken place there, and a former film queen is now the reigning princess. The famous and the rich have spent their leisure here; Winston Churchill, for example, loved to paint and to relax in those hills and at the Hotel de Paris.

There is a cafe in the main square where we sit in the open, having our mid-day snack to the accompaniment of Hungarian violins, and talk over the hands from the bridge festival. Here is one about which I was very happy to talk. North dealt at love all:

<pre>
                    ♠ K, Q, 7
                    ♡ A, 3
                    ◇ 6, 5
                    ♣ A, K, 10, 8, 7, 5
</pre>

<pre>
♠ 9, 6, 5, 4   ♠ A, J, 10, 3, 2
♡ Q, 9   ┌──────────┐   ♡ 8, 7, 5, 4
◇ A, J, 10, 8   │   N   │   ◇ 3, 2
♣ Q, 4, 2   W│   E │   ♣ J, 6
                   │   S   │
                   └──────────┘
</pre>

<pre>
                    ♠ 8
                    ♡ K, J, 10, 6, 2
                    ◇ K, Q, 9, 7, 4
                    ♣ 9, 3
</pre>

The bidding may have played some part in my achievement:

North	East	South	West
1♣	NB	1♡	NB
3♣	NB	3◇	Double
3NT	NB	4♡	NB
NB	NB		

Sitting South I did not like 3NT unless partner could bid 3♠ over 3◇. He was marked with some fit in hearts.

West led the 4 of spades. I played the queen from dummy and East the ace. A diamond came back; I played the king and West took the trick with the ace. West then played a low club, and I realised as I took it that I was going to be cut off from the club suit by lack of entries. I also had to cope with the trump situation; I placed East with four trumps, and if he held the queen I could never catch it. I played the ace of trumps, and when I saw West's 9 drop I decided to play him for Q, 9 doubleton. I could now see my way to two club tricks, one spade trick, one diamond trick and five trump tricks. Whence the tenth?

Before drawing any more trumps I played another club to

52

test that suit; then I ruffed the third round of clubs with the 10 of trumps, cashed the queen of diamonds and jack of trumps, discarding dummy's low spade, and threw East in with the 8 of trumps to lead up to my spade and so let me cash my club winners.

A long argument followed: West reproached East for not returning the jack of spades at trick two. This would not have made my task more difficult. I would have drawn four rounds of trumps, given up a club trick and come to ten tricks this way. The only clever defence would have been for West not to take the ace of diamonds at trick two. But even then they could not have beaten me. I would have drawn all the trumps, played the ace and king of clubs and ruffed a club; then a low diamond. West could have cashed two diamonds but then would have had to play a spade or let me make my diamonds for ten tricks.

In fact the defence forced me into an unusual play whereby I had to set up a trump winner for them in exchange for an entry to dummy for my winners.

"Oh, very well played, Rixi," said my friends. "Now tell us how you made only ten tricks when everyone else made eleven in 4♡ on. . . ." My friends, did I say? I couldn't escape and here it is: South dealt at love all:

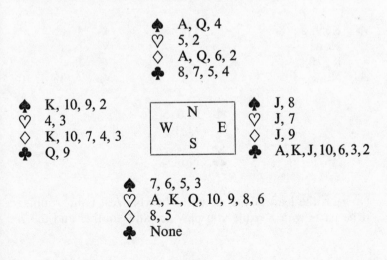

	♠ A, Q, 4	
	♡ 5, 2	
	◇ A, Q, 6, 2	
	♣ 8, 7, 5, 4	

♠ K, 10, 9, 2		♠ J, 8
♡ 4, 3	N	♡ J, 7
◇ K, 10, 7, 4, 3	W E	◇ J, 9
♣ Q, 9	S	♣ A, K, J, 10, 6, 3, 2

	♠ 7, 6, 5, 3	
	♡ A, K, Q, 10, 9, 8, 6	
	◇ 8, 5	
	♣ None	

I opened 4♥, which silenced everyone at the table. West led the 10 of spades and I immediately got the *idée fixe* that East had ♠ K, J bare, so I played the ace and East dropped the 8. I drew trumps, successfully finessed the queen of diamonds and returned to hand by trumping a club. Then I led a low spade, and when West played low, I played low from dummy! I now had to lose three spade tricks.

"I know," I said, "I must have been mad. How could East possibly have ♠ K, J bare when he played the 8 on the first trick? As West had led the 10, East had the jack and 8 and might or might not hold the king. I could not lose by playing the queen. East could have made it more difficult by following the principle of playing the card you are known to hold – the jack in this case – on the first trick."

Worse was to come from my friends.

"You can make 6♥ for a top," they pointed out. "Finesse queen of spades, draw trumps, finesse queen of diamonds and rattle trumps to produce this ending:

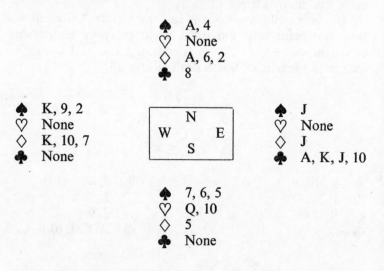

```
              ♠  A, 4
              ♥  None
              ◇  A, 6, 2
              ♣  8

♠ K, 9, 2        ┌─────────┐        ♠ J
♥ None           │    N    │        ♥ None
◇ K, 10, 7     W │         │ E      ◇ J
♣ None           │    S    │        ♣ A, K, J, 10
                 └─────────┘
              ♠  7, 6, 5
              ♥  Q, 10
              ◇  5
              ♣  None
```

Now on the lead of the queen of hearts West is in trouble. If he parts with a spade you play ace and another and the 7 becomes a winner; and if he elects to throw a diamond you can ruff the third diamond good."

"I must have been watching the boats go by," I replied shortly and quickly changed the subject.

I turned to Jean Besse and asked: "How did you make 4♠, Jean, on the hand where your partner held ♠ A, Q, 8 . . . ?"

"I remember. This was the hand, with North–South vulnerable and East the dealer:

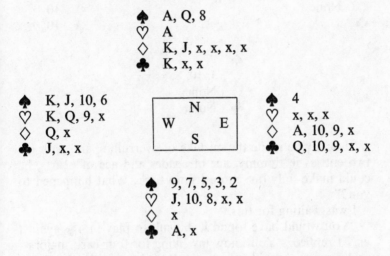

```
            ♠  A, Q, 8
            ♡  A
            ◇  K, J, x, x, x, x
            ♣  K, x, x

♠ K, J, 10, 6        N           ♠ 4
♡ K, Q, 9, x     W       E       ♡ x, x, x
◇ Q, x               S           ◇ A, 10, 9, x
♣ J, x, x                        ♣ Q, 10, 9, x, x

            ♠  9, 7, 5, 3, 2
            ♡  J, 10, 8, x, x
            ◇  x
            ♣  A, x
```

"My partner (North) likes to bid. He opened fourth in hand with 1◇, I bid a tentative spade and he forced with 3♣. I showed my second suit (!) with 3♡ and, of course, we had to reach 4♠. West led a low club and I didn't think much of our prospects. With so few entries to my own hand I decided to try and set up the diamond suit in dummy. I won the lead in hand and led a diamond, finessing the jack. East won with the ace and returned a club, taken by the king on the table. I played a low diamond, ruffing in hand, which felled West's queen. Crossing to dummy by way of the spade finesse I led another diamond and again ruffed low. There was nothing West could do – this was the position with West still to play:

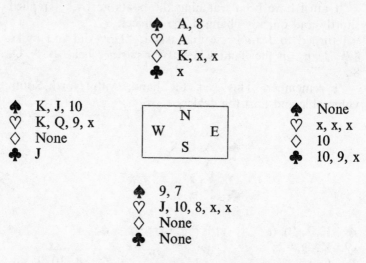

♠ A, 8
♡ A
◇ K, x, x
♣ x

♠ K, J, 10   ♠ None
♡ K, Q, 9, x   ♡ x, x, x
◇ None   ◇ 10
♣ J   ♣ 10, 9, x

♠ 9, 7
♡ J, 10, 8, x, x
◇ None
♣ None

"Luckily he made the mistake of overruffing and with my two entries in dummy, ace of spades and ace of hearts, he could make only one more trump trick. What happened to you?"

I was waiting for this.

"You would have found it difficult to play in 4♠ against us," I replied. "You know my liking for four-card majors – so I opened the bidding on the West hand with 1♠, North bid 2◇, my partner passed, South bid 2♡ and North hastily converted to 2NT, which was passed out. My darling partner led a club and we held declarer to five tricks: + 300 for us."

I wonder no waiter has thought of having the menus bound and producing a book on French Cookery and Continental Bridge, for the *plats du jour* generally seem to consist of ball-point spades, hearts, diamonds and clubs.

I don't know much about wild-fowling in Monte Carlo,

but this hand certainly produced a skein of ducks. South
dealt at game all:

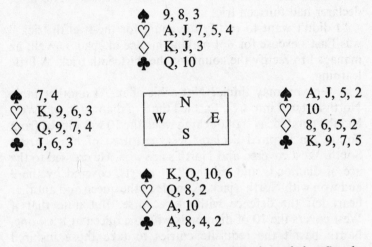

♠ 9, 8, 3
♡ A, J, 7, 5, 4
◇ K, J, 3
♣ Q, 10

♠ 7, 4
♡ K, 9, 6, 3
◇ Q, 9, 7, 4
♣ J, 6, 3

♠ A, J, 5, 2
♡ 10
◇ 8, 6, 5, 2
♣ K, 9, 7, 5

♠ K, Q, 10, 6
♡ Q, 8, 2
◇ A, 10
♣ A, 8, 4, 2

At our table my partner, Jonathan Cansino, sitting South,
opened 1NT. I introduced a Stayman bid of 2♣, asking my
partner if he had a four-card major, and when he covered my
spade weakness by bidding 2♠, I settled for 3NT.

West led the 6 of hearts. He had decided that I held a
heart suit (I was dummy, of course), so he was trying a small
diversion at trick one. Not diverted, South played low from
dummy, won East's 10 with the queen, and continued with
the 2 of hearts. When West followed with the 3, he inserted the
5 from dummy (from his play of the 10 East was marked
with the king or a singleton), and East discarded a diamond.
Declarer now led a low spade from dummy, East also played
low and the king won. Dummy was entered by way of the
heart finesse and the long hearts cashed, East parting with
more diamonds. The 8 of spades was next played from North,
and when East played the 5 it was allowed to run. When
a further spade was now led from dummy East (incredibly)
ducked again and declarer's queen won. He followed with

the ace of diamonds and the diamond finesse, and when the king of diamonds was cashed in dummy, East had to part with either his ace of spades or a club. Whatever he decided, declarer had thirteen tricks.

"I didn't want to rectify the count for the twelfth trick," was East's excuse for not making his ace of spades. Well, he managed to rectify the count for the thirteenth trick. A little learning. . . .

A top you may think? Not a bit of it. At another table North tottered into 6♡. East led the 8 of diamonds and West had the good idea (!) of ducking when the 10 was played from South. An inspired declarer led the queen of hearts from South, West covered and North's ace won. He crossed to the ace of diamonds and led the 8 of hearts, covered by the 9 and won with North's jack. A spade to the queen and another heart left the defence without recourse. But note that if West covers the 10 of diamonds with the queen at trick one, North hasn't the requisite entries to take those inspired trump finesses. He will try for two entries in spades, but East will take the second spade with the ace and give West a ruff.

But the funniest "duckment" of all was when South, owing to a misunderstanding, had passed 4♣ doubled (forcing!) and was left to play there. A spade was led, East ducked and South won with the 10. He now led a club to the 10 in dummy. And East? He ducked, of course. The queen of clubs followed, East played low, and so (surprise!) did declarer. After a little more manoeuvring declarer made the 8 of trumps *en passant* and garnered eleven tricks in all.

We've heard of wild ducks, but this is ridiculous.

The Monte Carlo Festival starts with an Individual event over five sessions. Here is a hand from this event which was defended in a masterly fashion by Mrs Durran, sitting West.

South dealt at game all:

```
              ♠ Q, x, x, x, x
              ♡ A, x
              ◇ x, x
              ♣ 10, x, x, x

♠ A, x                        ♠ J, 10, 9, x
♡ x, x          N             ♡ J, x, x
◇ A, K, Q, 10, x, x  W   E    ◇ J, x, x
♣ x, x, x            S        ♣ K, x, x

              ♠ K, x
              ♡ K, Q, 10, 9, x, x
              ◇ x, x
              ♣ A, Q, J
```

Bidding:

South	West	North	East
1♡	3◇	NB	NB
3♡	NB	4♡	NB
NB	NB		

West led the king of diamonds and East played the 2.

At this stage the play of a low card merely indicates an odd number of cards in the suit; this often helps partner and rarely does any harm. West now cashed her second diamond winner and led a trump. Whatever her partner's trump holding was, this lead could not help declarer, who was marked with at least six hearts: after West's 3◇ bid even the queen to three would be easily discovered. Declarer played low in dummy and took the trick in his own hand, returned to dummy with the ace of trumps and played the club finesse. Again East played the 2. West now correctly placed her partner with three diamonds and three clubs and either five spades and two hearts or – which seemed more likely – four spades and three hearts.

59

Declarer took another round of hearts and here came the crucial play; declarer led a low spade from his own hand. West played the ace and continued with a diamond, and now declarer could not enter dummy again to finesse for the second time against East's king of clubs. North said to his partner: "You should have led the king of spades," but Mrs Durran chipped in: "I would not have taken it." The king could not have been a singleton because if it were declarer would have played it before removing the ace of trumps from dummy.

The defence thus came to two diamond tricks, one spade and one club trick for a score of + 100.

When experts congregate they like to boast about living dangerously, particularly in individual events. Dr Chodziesner told us of this example of sheer low cunning. He was sitting South and North dealt at love all:

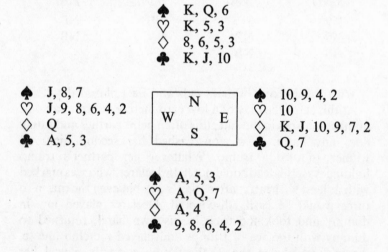

```
                    ♠ K, Q, 6
                    ♡ K, 5, 3
                    ◇ 8, 6, 5, 3
                    ♣ K, J, 10

♠ J, 8, 7              N            ♠ 10, 9, 4, 2
♡ J, 9, 8, 6, 4, 2  W   E          ♡ 10
◇ Q                   S            ◇ K, J, 10, 9, 7, 2
♣ A, 5, 3                          ♣ Q, 7

                    ♠ A, 5, 3
                    ♡ A, Q, 7
                    ◇ A, 4
                    ♣ 9, 8, 6, 4, 2
```

Dr Chodziesner's "Individual" partner had proved himself on the two previous boards to be more adept at light opening bids than at dummy play. He opened 1♣ and East overcalled 1◇. Dr Chodziesner, not wishing to confuse his partner with scientific bidding, and anxious to ensure that he played the hand himself, bid 3NT.

West led the queen of diamonds. East overtook with the king and continued diamonds, South winning the second trick. It was obvious that if East had the ace of clubs the contract was unmakable, and if West held the ace and queen the contract was cold. But what if West held the ace and East the queen?

Declarer crossed to dummy with a spade and led the jack of clubs with the air of a man about to play the ace on it and finesse dummy's K, 10 for the queen. Poor East, whose only chance of an entry was the queen of clubs, had to hope that South *was* a man who would play the ace and finesse on the next round, so he played low. West ducked, but declarer had the answer to this; he crossed over to his own hand with a heart and played another club. West ducked again, but declarer played dummy's king, felling East's queen. The rest was easy – 3NT made with two overtricks.

When Dr Chodziesner recounted this to us the reaction was: "You were lucky, not that East didn't cover your jack of clubs with the queen – that was difficult for him – but that West didn't make the obvious (sic) play of discarding his ace of clubs on the second diamond. If he had counted his own, dummy's and declarer's presumed (13 or 14) points, he would have realised that there was hardly room for East to have a quick entry."

"Ah, but if you are going to defend in that manner, I shall take the first diamond trick and not give West a chance to discard his ace of clubs," replied Chody. "Perhaps I should have taken the first diamond anyway," he added reflectively.

July
Deauville

Deauville has established itself as the most important bridge centre in Europe, and almost all July is devoted to the International Bridge Festival.

After a pleasant and amusing gathering of friends the festival crescendos to a mass open event at the Casino, where hundreds of players compete for the many wonderful gifts and money prizes. Among the attractions are the magnificent Olympic swimming pool, with heated filtered seawater and one part open to the blue skies; the bridge-golf tournament; and the Tournament of Champions, which can be watched on Bridgerama, with expert commentators reviewing the bidding and play of the world's best players.

Princess Nadine of Lichtenstein, also well known as the French International Nadine Ansay, creates an atmosphere of glamour and efficiency which lends a great deal of prestige to all the events she promotes. The most important encounters under her patronage are the Cannes Festival in Spring and the meeting at Deauville in July. Each of these festivals is preceded by an intimate gathering of her personal friends for a *semaine de bridge* – a *tournée privée* for which you require a special invitation.

At this event, the main programme comprises an Individual, a Mixed Pairs and a Patton for Teams of Four. It is held at the very comfortable Hotel du Golf, and for the golfers there is a bridge-golf competition. The non-golfers can take part in a gin-rummy contest. This is one of the most enjoyable weeks: only a few experts are admitted, everybody knows everybody and at least half of the 100 competitors receive wonderful prizes.

There is a twofold satisfaction for the spectator of Bridgerama: first, the satisfaction of seeing the experts execute manoeuvres and plays which would have been beyond his own capacity; and, secondly, the consolation of seeing occasional signs of fallibility among the great. There was something of both these pleasures in the following hand, dealt by East at game all:

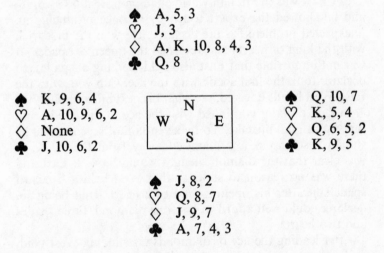

♠ A, 5, 3
♡ J, 3
◇ A, K, 10, 8, 4, 3
♣ Q, 8

♠ K, 9, 6, 4
♡ A, 10, 9, 6, 2
◇ None
♣ J, 10, 6, 2

♠ Q, 10, 7
♡ K, 5, 4
◇ Q, 6, 5, 2
♣ K, 9, 5

♠ J, 8, 2
♡ Q, 8, 7
◇ J, 9, 7
♣ A, 7, 4, 3

The bidding:

East	South	West	North
NB	NB	NB	1◇
NB	1NT	Double	NB
NB	NB		

The hasty analysts were inclined to criticise West's double of 1NT, suggesting 2◇ as a more acceptable alternative. West (Egyptian film star Omar Sharif) had reasoned better than his critics. The objection, he said, to 2◇ (asking for a major suit) was that it precluded the possibility of playing in 2♣. The double of 1NT could not be construed as other than distributional: how could a hand which had passed originally hold the high-card strength for a penalty double of 1NT when the strength of the hand on his left was still unlimited?

Against 1NT doubled West led the 10 of hearts and declarer's prospects looked bright. A heart continuation seemed likely and that would give him one heart trick, at least five diamonds, and the two black aces.

But East was the Italian world champion Benito Garozzo, and he showed the expert touch by at once producing an unexpected problem for the declarer. He won the first trick with the king of hearts and returned the queen of spades. It was not impossible that East also held the king of spades, so declarer took the first spade with the ace. Can you, with the East–West hands covered, see what his next move should be?

In fact, declarer continued with the ace of diamonds, and that was a fatal mistake. To make certain of seven tricks, he should first play a low diamond away from the A, K. It was clear that the diamond length would be with East and there was no reason to suppose that West held a five-card spade suit after his opening lead of a heart. That being so, declarer could well afford to lose one diamond, three spades and two hearts.

After leading the ace of diamonds and finding West void, declarer continued with a low diamond towards the jack, which East allowed to win. There was now no point in setting up the diamonds by conceding a trick to East, for declarer's only possible entry to the long cards was the queen of clubs (if, as might be hoped, the king was in the doubler's hand on his left), and that would entail far too many losers. Declarer therefore tried to set up the queen of clubs immediately, which would give him three diamonds, one spade, one heart and two club tricks. However, the queen of clubs lost to the king and East continued spades, and when West led the thirteenth spade declarer was obliged to part with a club. West now switched to the jack of clubs and was able to take two more club tricks and the ace of hearts for two down.

Jean Besse is always good value to watch on Bridgerama. His speed of analysis confounds the speaker, the commentator, the opposition and the spectators – as witness this hand, dealt by East with East–West vulnerable:

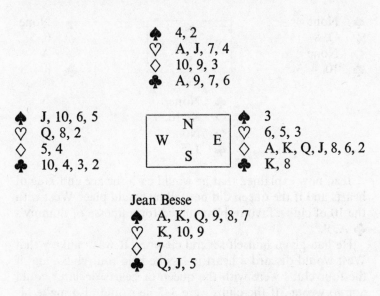

```
              ♠  4, 2
              ♡  A, J, 7, 4
              ◇  10, 9, 3
              ♣  A, 9, 7, 6

♠  J, 10, 6, 5          N          ♠  3
♡  Q, 8, 2         W         E     ♡  6, 5, 3
◇  5, 4                 S          ◇  A, K, Q, J, 8, 6, 2
♣  10, 4, 3, 2                     ♣  K, 8

              Jean Besse
              ♠  A, K, Q, 9, 8, 7
              ♡  K, 10, 9
              ◇  7
              ♣  Q, J, 5
```

East opened a conventional 1♣, South bid 2♠ and North made a good raise to 4♠. (East–West were Bianchi and Messina, who play the "Livorno Diamond". A bid of 1◇ in that system shows a much stronger hand.)

West led a diamond. Declarer (Jean Besse) ruffed the second round and played two rounds of trumps, East discarding a diamond on the second round. Declarer then led the queen of clubs and ran it to East's king. East continued with diamonds, ruffed by declarer and overruffed by West, who exited with a trump. North discarded a heart and East another diamond. On declarer's last trump West discarded the 2 of hearts, North the jack of hearts and East yet another diamond.

This was the position:

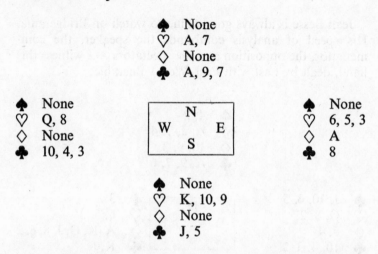

```
                    ♠ None
                    ♡ A, 7
                    ◇ None
                    ♣ A, 9, 7

♠ None                             ♠ None
♡ Q, 8          N                  ♡ 6, 5, 3
◇ None      W       E              ◇ A
♣ 10, 4, 3      S                  ♣ 8

                    ♠ None
                    ♡ K, 10, 9
                    ◇ None
                    ♣ J, 5
```

Jean now explained that he would cash the ace and king of hearts and if the queen did not fall he would place West with the 10 of clubs, favourably situated for a finesse of dummy's ♣ A, 9.

He had given himself several chances. It was unlikely that West would discard a heart unless he held four clubs, and if the four clubs were with the queen of hearts declarer could not go wrong. If the clubs were 3–3 he would also make his contract. Besse is a very fine mathematician and works the odds out to perfection. I am not, but I was most impressed by his logic.

The American partnership, Roth and Stone, always give a good account of themselves. Mr Stone had problems on the following hand. I don't pretend to understand their system, but they reached 6♢ :

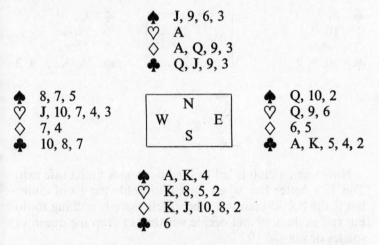

♠ J, 9, 6, 3
♡ A
♢ A, Q, 9, 3
♣ Q, J, 9, 3

♠ 8, 7, 5
♡ J, 10, 7, 4, 3
♢ 7, 4
♣ 10, 8, 7

♠ Q, 10, 2
♡ Q, 9, 6
♢ 6, 5
♣ A, K, 5, 4, 2

♠ A, K, 4
♡ K, 8, 5, 2
♢ K, J, 10, 8, 2
♣ 6

West led the jack of hearts, won in dummy with the ace. Declarer drew one round of trumps and then led a club to the queen and East's ace (an automatic false card in this position). East continued with a heart, won with the king, and declarer cashed the ace and king of spades, hoping for the queen to drop. When this failed he entered dummy with a trump and led the jack of clubs. East did not cover and South discarded his losing spade. You will see that it makes no difference whether East covers or not: if he does, South ruffs, trumps a heart in dummy and trumps another club, felling West's 10, and he still has another heart ruff to enter dummy for the winning 9 of clubs.

As I watched the hand being played on Bridgerama I wondered whether a partial elimination might be a better play. Draw two rounds of trumps, cash the king of hearts, ruff a heart and cash one top spade, leaving this position:

```
              ♠ J, 9
              ♡ None
              ◇ 9
              ♣ Q, J, 9, 3
```

```
♠ 8, 7                              ♠ Q, 10
♡ 10, 7          N                  ♡ None
◇ None       W       E              ◇ None
♣ 10, 8, 7       S                  ♣ A, K, 5, 4, 2

              ♠ K, 4
              ♡ 8
              ◇ K, J, 10
              ♣ 6
```

Now when a club is led to East he cannot find a safe exit. This is a better line when East also holds the 10 of clubs, but if the horrid man has a heart left there is nothing to do but ruff in dummy and decide whether to drop the queen of spades or pin the 10.

When giants cross swords it is always good to watch, and here John Collings and Terence Reese brought off a good double-cross in defence against Forquet and Garozzo of the famous Italian Blue Team. West dealt with North–South vulnerable:

```
              ♠ A, 10, 7, 5, 3
              ♡ 4
              ◇ Q, J, 10, 5, 3
              ♣ J, 9
```

```
♠ 9, 8, 6, 4                          ♠ Q, J
♡ 5, 3, 2          N                  ♡ J, 10, 9, 8, 7, 6
◇ 4, 2         W       E              ◇ A, 8, 7
♣ 10, 4, 3, 2      S                  ♣ K, 8

              ♠ K, 2
              ♡ A, K, Q
              ◇ K, 9, 6
              ♣ A, Q, 7, 6, 5
```

After West and North had passed, East (John Collings) started the ball rolling with an opening bid of 3♡, and South (Garozzo) finally played in 6NT. West led a heart, won by declarer, who now played on diamonds. Collings held up his ace until the third round, on which West discarded a heart, and then switched to the queen of spades, South winning in hand with the king. Declarer now cashed his top hearts, and Reese (West) cunningly discarded a low spade. Garozzo was thus faced with this problem: had East started life with six hearts, three diamonds, three clubs and a singleton spade? After making a pre-emptive bid he had already shown up with the ace of diamonds and the queen of spades, so it seemed that West must hold the king of clubs. If both these inferences were correct, West could be squeezed by the play of the winning diamonds after a spade finesse, because this is the position that would develop:

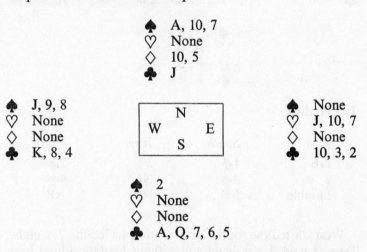

	♠	A, 10, 7
	♡	None
	◇	10, 5
	♣	J

♠ J, 9, 8		♠ None
♡ None	N	♡ J, 10, 7
◇ None	W E	◇ None
♣ K, 8, 4	S	♣ 10, 3, 2

	♠	2
	♡	None
	◇	None
	♣	A, Q, 7, 6, 5

Declarer therefore finessed the 10 of spades and went four down on his contract. At the other tables East opened only 1♡ and declarer had no difficulty in placing the missing face cards. The trouble with John Collings's pre-empts, like the famous Adam Meredith's, is that they may consist of anything from a three-card to a seven-card suit and any number of points between none and what-have-you.

Experts can make mistakes, and like lesser mortals they make more in defence than elsewhere. The true master is the one who gives the defence a chance to go wrong and then sees to it that there is no recovery for them. And talking of Terence Reese, see on this hand how he bemused the defence. East dealt at love all:

```
              ♠ Q, 9, 7
              ♡ 2
              ◇ Q, 7, 4, 3
              ♣ A, Q, 9, 8, 3

♠ None                              ♠ K, J, 10, 3, 2
♡ K, J, 10, 9, 4     N              ♡ Q, 8, 7
◇ A, J, 9, 6, 5, 2  W   E           ◇ 10
♣ 7, 6                  S           ♣ J, 10, 5, 2

              ♠ A, 8, 6, 5, 4
              ♡ A, 6, 5, 3
              ◇ K, 8
              ♣ K, 4
```

The bidding:

East	South	West	North
NB	1♠	2♡	2♠
3♡	3♠	NB	4♠
Double	NB	NB	NB

West started the rot for his side when he led the 7 of clubs. Terence won this in hand and without hesitation fired back the 8 of diamonds. Incredibly West ducked and the queen won in dummy. The ace and queen of clubs were cashed, declarer discarding the king of diamonds, and when West also discarded the trump position became clear. Timing his play very carefully, declarer cashed the ace of hearts and ruffed a heart in dummy, a club in his own hand and another heart in dummy.

This was now the position, declarer having made all eight tricks:

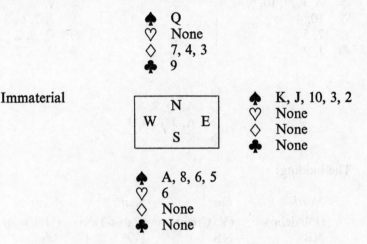

```
              ♠  Q
              ♡  None
              ◇  7, 4, 3
              ♣  9

Immaterial          N              ♠  K, J, 10, 3, 2
              W          E         ♡  None
                     S             ◇  None
                                   ♣  None

              ♠  A, 8, 6, 5
              ♡  6
              ◇  None
              ♣  None
```

Declarer led the 9 of clubs from dummy, East ruffed with the jack and South overruffed with the ace. He now led his last heart, ruffed in dummy with the queen. East won with the king of trumps – but could do no better now than cash his 10 and give declarer the last two tricks with 8 and 6 for one doubled overtrick.

Charming and amusing Camillo Pabis-Ticci does not need any introduction to the world's bridge players. He is a star among stars and, of course, a member of the Italian Blue Team. Here is an example of his skill as he avoided a trap laid by the Formosan champion, Professor H. Chen. North dealt at game all:

71

```
                    ♠  Q, 2
                    ♡  K, 9, 2
                    ◇  K, 10, 6
                    ♣  Q, 10, 8, 6, 3
```

```
♠  A, K, J, 10, 6, 4, 3  ┌─────────────┐   ♠  9, 8
♡  10, 4                 │      N      │   ♡  J, 7, 6, 3
◇  7, 5                  │  W       E  │   ◇  Q, 9, 2
♣  J, 9                  │      S      │   ♣  A, 7, 5, 2
                         └─────────────┘
```

```
                    ♠  7, 5
                    ♡  A, Q, 8, 5
                    ◇  A, J, 8, 4, 3
                    ♣  K, 4
```

The bidding:

North	East	South	West
(D'Alelio)	(V. Chen)	(Pabis-Ticci)	(H. Chen)
NB	NB	1♡	3♠
4♡	NB	NB	NB

West cashed the ace and king of spades and continued
with the jack, which declarer ruffed in dummy, discarding
the low club from his own hand. East also discarded a club,
and when declarer led one from table he went in with the
ace and continued the suit. Declarer discarded a diamond
from hand and won the trick in dummy, noting from West's
play of the jack and the 9 that the clubs in dummy were
now winners. West was counted for seven spades and two
clubs originally – what were his four red cards? If East held
five hearts or J, 10, x, x, declarer could not make the contract. What further clues could he pick up? With four diamonds East might well have discarded one instead of a

club; with three hearts including the jack or 10 he might have overruffed dummy. So Pabis-Ticci led a heart to his ace, cashed his ace of diamonds and led a heart to the king on table, noting the fall of West's 10. This was now the position with the lead in dummy:

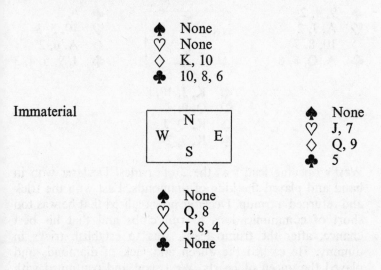

♠ None
♡ None
◇ K, 10
♣ 10, 8, 6

Immaterial

```
    N
W       E
    S
```

♠ None
♡ J, 7
◇ Q, 9
♣ 5

♠ None
♡ Q, 8
◇ J, 8, 4
♣ None

The 10 of clubs was led, South discarding a diamond, followed by the 8 and East was helpless; if he ruffed, declarer would overruff, draw the last trump and return to dummy with the king of diamonds to cash the last club, and if he discarded, declarer would remain in dummy to "coup" his trumps at the twelfth trick.

I saw another champion play the same way to trick five, but then he played the king of trumps first and therefore lacked a vital entry in dummy for the "coup".

Although during the *semaine de bridge privée* bridge itself is not taken too seriously, everybody is interested in a well-played hand. The one below was played by Prince Lichtenstein (the president of the Austrian Bridge Federation) in 4♠:

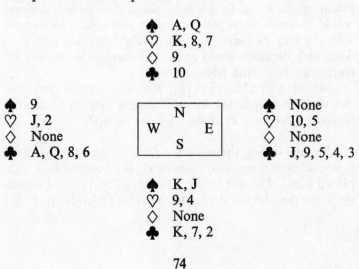

```
                    ♠ A, Q, 7, 5
                    ♡ K, 8, 7, 6
                    ◇ 9, 5, 4, 3
                    ♣ 10
♠ 9, 4, 2                              ♠ 6, 3
♡ A, J, 2          N                   ♡ 10, 5, 3
◇ 10, 8, 7     W       E               ◇ A, 6, 2
♣ A, Q, 8, 6       S                   ♣ J, 9, 5, 4, 3
                    ♠ K, J, 10, 8
                    ♡ Q, 9, 4
                    ◇ K, Q, J
                    ♣ K, 7, 2
```

West's opening lead was the 2 of spades. Declarer won in
hand and played the king of diamonds. East won the trick
and returned a trump. Declarer now realised that he was too
short of communications to ruff clubs and that his best
chance, after the trump leads, was to establish tricks in
dummy. He cashed the queen and jack of diamonds and
played the queen of hearts. West won and continued with
trumps. This was the position at trick 7:

```
                    ♠ A, Q
                    ♡ K, 8, 7
                    ◇ 9
                    ♣ 10
♠ 9                                    ♠ None
♡ J, 2             N                   ♡ 10, 5
◇ None         W       E               ◇ None
♣ A, Q, 8, 6       S                   ♣ J, 9, 5, 4, 3
                    ♠ K, J
                    ♡ 9, 4
                    ◇ None
                    ♣ K, 7, 2
```

Dummy's ace of trumps won the trick. Prince Lichtenstein discarded a heart on the 9 of diamonds and played the king and another heart, ruffing in hand with his last trump. A club was given up to the defenders but nothing could now stop 10 tricks. Declarer lost only the ace of diamonds, the ace of hearts and a club trick.

In the other room, on the same lead, declarer made the mistake of leading a club from dummy at the second trick. When the defenders got in with the ace of diamonds they forced dummy with a club and declarer found himself unable to ruff two clubs, draw trumps, make the long diamond and get out the ace of hearts.

The Champions' Tournament in Deauville in 1971 was won by Britain's young players, Jonathan Cansino and Bob Sheehan. Most of the eight pairs who competed in this "Special Event" played artificial systems, and once more it was shown that in the slam-bidding department the Blue Club system (a variation of the Neapolitan Club specially tailored for the "Omar Sharif Circus"), coped better than the others. Here are three hands on which Omar and his partner sailed into slam contracts where most of the other pairs got their wires crossed:

Sharif
♠ Q, 7, 5
♡ A, K, Q, 6
♢ Q, 10, 3, 2
♣ 4, 3

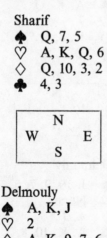

Delmouly
♠ A, K, J
♡ 2
♢ A, K, 9, 7, 6, 5
♣ A, Q, J

75

Bidding: *South*   *North*

1♣[1]	1♠[2]
2◇	2♡
3◇	4◇
4♡[3]	5♡[4]
6◇[5]	NB

[1] 17 points or more.
[2] 3 controls and forcing to game. The next bids are natural and diamonds is the agreed suit.
[3] Showing the singleton.
[4] This indicates no top values in spades or clubs; therefore the 3 controls should be in hearts.
[5] A lazy bid because South can now be practically sure of 13 tricks.

On the next hand two Precision Club pairs failed to reach even 6♠ when 7♠ could not be beaten. Below is the sequence by which Delmouly and Sharif bid the small slam:

Sharif
♠ A, K, Q
♡ 7
◇ K, 8, 6, 5, 4, 2
♣ Q, 7, 5

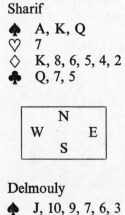

Delmouly
♠ J, 10, 9, 7, 6, 3
♡ None
◇ A, J
♣ A, K, 10, 8, 3

Bidding:

South	West	North	East
1♠	2♡	3◇	NB
3♠	NB	4♡	NB
5♣	NB	5♠	NB
6♠	NB	NB	NB

It is not easy to locate the queen of clubs, but I am bold enough to say that with natural systems it would be very easy to get to 6♠ and even 7♠.

There are two possible sequences, one with and one without intervention.

The first is:

South	West	North	East
1♠	2♡	3♡	NB
4♣	NB	4♠	NB
5♡	NB	6♣	NB
6◇	NB	7♠	NB
NB	NB		

The second is:

South	West	North	East
1♠	NB	3◇	NB
4♣	NB	4♠	NB
5◇	NB	5♡	NB
6♡	NB	7♠	NB
NB	NB		

The next one was bid only by Delmouly and Sharif. Dealer North:

Delmouly
- ♠ K, 7, 3
- ♡ 9, 5, 3, 2
- ◇ 8, 7, 6, 4, 2
- ♣ K

```
        N
   W         E
        S
```

Sharif
- ♠ A, 10, 8, 6
- ♡ A, K, 8, 7, 6, 4
- ◇ Q
- ♣ A, 10

North	West	South	East
NB	NB	1♣[1]	NB
1♡[2]	NB	2♡[3]	NB
3♡[4]	NB	3♠[5]	NB
4♣[6]	NB	4◇[7]	NB
4♠[8]	NB	6♡	NB
NB	NB		

[1] 17 points or more.
[2] 6 points or more.
[3] This is my suit.
[4] I am with you.
[5] Shows control.
[6] Not more than one loser.
[7] The same.
[8] I am with you in spades.

Sharif correctly came to the conclusion that his partner's encouraging bids should make 6♡ a good bet. As North's hand has mainly distributional values it might not be too easy to reach the slam without using cue bids or a control-showing device like asking bids – a convention that I have found extremely useful for slam bidding. I have never understood why it is not used by more players.

Reese and Flint reached a difficult 6♣ contract on these two hands:

Reese
♠ 3
♡ A, K, 10, 7, 2
◇ Q, 8, 7
♣ K, Q, 10, 6

Flint
♠ A, Q, J, 6, 2
♡ Q, 3
◇ None
♣ J, 8, 7, 5, 3, 2

South	North
1♠	2♡
3♣	3◇
3♡	4♣
4◇	6♣

This is a hand on which one could normally reach the slam only by using a comparatively new method. I believe that some of the Italian systems employ it. I do so too with some partners. I would suggest the following sequence:

South	North
NB	1♡
1♠	2♣
4◇[1]	4♡
6♣	

[1] Showing a perfect fit in clubs and first-round control in diamonds.

79

August
Miscellany

There are no international bridge festivals in August – the month when I generally take a holiday from competitive bridge, and indeed only play carefree rubber bridge occasionally. So perhaps this is a good time to look back on some events which are not open to everyone.

The *Sunday Times* Pairs Championship might be called the blue riband of invitation pairs. It is run by the British Bridge League, who invite international aces to London to compete against each other. The event was won in 1971 by Bob Slavenburg (Holland) and Leon Tintner (France), with Omar Sharif and Benito Garozzo, who had led the field of experts through most of the five sessions, finishing second.

I suppose one could say that in the final analysis the result turned on the pip-blindness of some weary opponents of the two winning pairs. On the following hand against the winners declarer went down in his slam contract, and against the runners-up declarer, not under pressure, made three overtricks in 3NT. In fact at all tables where the contract was 3NT twelve tricks were made and at the other tables where the contract was 5♣, 6♣ or 6NT only eleven tricks rolled home. West dealt at love all:

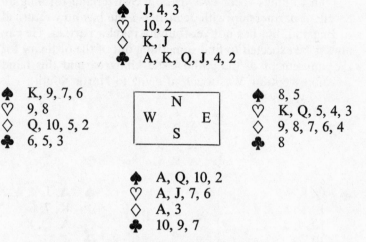

♠ J, 4, 3
♡ 10, 2
◇ K, J
♣ A, K, Q, J, 4, 2

♠ K, 9, 7, 6
♡ 9, 8
◇ Q, 10, 5, 2
♣ 6, 5, 3

♠ 8, 5
♡ K, Q, 5, 4, 3
◇ 9, 8, 7, 6, 4
♣ 8

♠ A, Q, 10, 2
♡ A, J, 7, 6
◇ A, 3
♣ 10, 9, 7

Where North played the contract in 6♣ or 6NT East led a top heart, and when South was declarer in 6NT West led the 9 of hearts. You will see that when play follows a normal route declarer will eventually lead the 10 of hearts to clear the queen for his jack to give him eleven tricks, with the intention of taking the spade finesse for his twelfth. The less pressurised declarers in 3NT noticed the fall of the 9 and 8 of hearts and gladly cashed the 7 for their third overtrick. The declarers who really needed to be alert missed those important pips, took the spade finesse and went down.

I was not able to find out how every table played the hand, but it may be that the clubs were rattled off with the hope that a squeeze would develop or that a defender could be thrown in with the heart honour to lead into the spade tenace. In this case, of course, South would eventually have to part with that precious 7 of hearts before the 9 and 8 were shown to be doubleton in the West hand.

I have to say, however, that the standard of play was excellent; it was only towards the end of this gruelling five-session event that tiredness occasioned a few errors.

John Collings spent two years in Switzerland forming an excellent partnership with Jean Besse. He has now returned to England, but has not yet found a regular partner. He can always be expected to find something out of the ordinary for the amusement of the enthusiastic kibitzers, and this hand was no exception. West dealt at game to North–South:

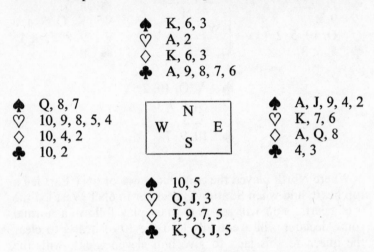

♠ K, 6, 3
♡ A, 2
♢ K, 6, 3
♣ A, 9, 8, 7, 6

♠ Q, 8, 7
♡ 10, 9, 8, 5, 4
♢ 10, 4, 2
♣ 10, 2

♠ A, J, 9, 4, 2
♡ K, 7, 6
♢ A, Q, 8
♣ 4, 3

♠ 10, 5
♡ Q, J, 3
♢ J, 9, 7, 5
♣ K, Q, J, 5

John became declarer in 2♠ sitting West – yes, West. North opened 1NT and Jean Besse, as East, overcalled with 2♢, which was some sort of conventional Astro-type take-out bid, showing spades and another suit. John bid 2♠ and all passed. I am not recommending the bidding sequence, which got East-West into a strange contract; but having got there John Collings was able to show his skill in taking advantage of errors in defence.

North had an awkward lead and helped John's cause along by starting with a low trump. West won with the queen, led a low heart to the king and exited with a club. The defence took two clubs, two hearts and eventually a diamond, but in the end they had to lead another round of trumps or yield a ruff and discard, so West was able to take the spade finesse for eight tricks.

The next hand was a source of annoyance to some players, but the American internationals Arthur Robinson and Robert Jordan had no complaints. North dealt at game to East–West:

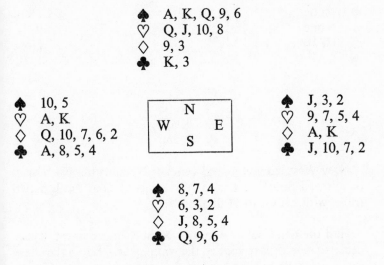

♠ A, K, Q, 9, 6
♡ Q, J, 10, 8
◇ 9, 3
♣ K, 3

♠ 10, 5
♡ A, K
◇ Q, 10, 7, 6, 2
♣ A, 8, 5, 4

♠ J, 3, 2
♡ 9, 7, 5, 4
◇ A, K
♣ J, 10, 7, 2

♠ 8, 7, 4
♡ 6, 3, 2
◇ J, 8, 5, 4
♣ Q, 9, 6

North opened 1♠ and after two passes, West (Jordan) bid 2◇. North tried 2♡ and East (Robinson) found the good bid of 3◇ which was passed all round.

North led three rounds of spades, West ruffing the third. From the bidding it was clear that North was likely to be short in diamonds and unlikely to hold both club honours; otherwise he might well have doubled instead of bidding 2♡. So playing on this assumption declarer immediately led a small club. North won with the king and found the only defence to cause declarer trouble: he continued with another spade. Dummy ruffed with the king and South discarded a club, but West had everything under control. He cashed the ace and king of hearts and ace of clubs, crossed to dummy with the ace of diamonds and ruffed a heart. This was now the position:

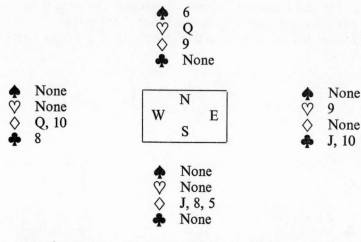

Now West led a club and whether North ruffed with his 9 or allowed South to trump, West had to take the last two tricks with his Q, 10 of diamonds.

Had the hand below been played in a "par contest" every declarer would have spotted the winning line, but in the chase for over-tricks many were left to justify themselves to censorious partners in the post-mortem. South dealt at game to North–South:

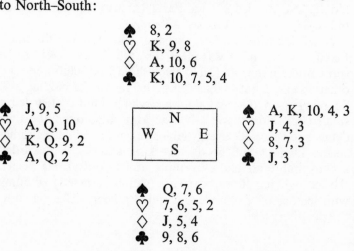

Against West's contract of 3NT North led the 5 of clubs and dummy's jack held the trick. Too often declarers now rushed to take the spade finesse and the clubs were cleared before they could set up red-suit winners. It is correct, of course, to take the heart finesse first into the "safe" hand, because if it loses North cannot profitably continue clubs; if he switches to a spade declarer must go up with dummy's ace and set up a diamond trick before taking the spade finesse. If North finds the good defence of holding up the king of hearts, then declarer must not relax and thoughtlessly take another heart finesse; he must now set up a diamond trick. Only at this point, with two heart tricks, two club tricks and one diamond trick in the bag, can declarer afford to finesse the spades. This is the sort of hand which, if I were a tournament director, I should like to pop into a board when there are a few know-it-all partnerships in operation!

This interesting hand was well played by the Polish international J. Wilkosz. West dealt at game all:

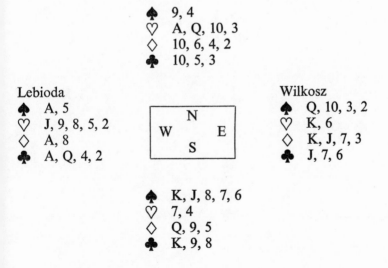

      ♠ 9, 4
      ♡ A, Q, 10, 3
      ◇ 10, 6, 4, 2
      ♣ 10, 5, 3

Lebioda
♠ A, 5
♡ J, 9, 8, 5, 2
◇ A, 8
♣ A, Q, 4, 2

   N
W   E
   S

Wilkosz
♠ Q, 10, 3, 2
♡ K, 6
◇ K, J, 7, 3
♣ J, 7, 6

      ♠ K, J, 8, 7, 6
      ♡ 7, 4
      ◇ Q, 9, 5
      ♣ K, 9, 8

West opened 1♡, East responded 1♠ and over West's rebid of 2♣ Wilkosz bid 2NT, raised to 3NT by his partner. At this stage North reckoned that East–West had nothing to spare for their bids and that things were lying badly for them, so he doubled.

Against 3NT doubled played by East, South led the 7 of hearts, North won with the ace and switched to the 9 of spades, covered by the 10, jack and ace. Declarer continued with a low club to the jack and king. He won the club return in dummy, cashed the king of hearts and dummy's two club winners and continued with the ace and king of diamonds. He then threw South in with a low diamond to the queen, forcing him to lead spades for the eighth trick, and the jack of diamonds made the ninth.

A well-played hand, but as it took thirty minutes to execute I was glad to move on and find high jinks and fun and games on these two hands.

South dealt the first one at game all:

```
                    ♠  A, K, 9, 4, 3, 2
                    ♡  5
                    ◇  A, K, 8, 4
                    ♣  K, J


 ♠  10, 8                    ┌─────────┐              ♠  7
 ♡  J, 10, 9, 8, 7, 2        │    N    │              ♡  A, K, Q, 4, 3
 ◇  Q, 9                     │ W     E │              ◇  6, 5, 2
 ♣  Q, 9, 6                  │    S    │              ♣  8, 7, 5, 4
                            └─────────┘


                    ♠  Q, J, 6, 5
                    ♡  6
                    ◇  J, 10, 7, 3
                    ♣  A, 10, 3, 2
```

There are so many internationals now playing variations of artificial club systems – and winning – that I am forced to the conclusion there must be something in them; or could it be that they are better bridge players and that's why they win? I am trying to keep an open mind, but I must confess that I had a chuckle or two at North–South's misfortunes on this little number.

Where North opened the bidding with 1♣, and that was a surprising number of times, East overcalled in hearts and South doubled. This is another convention that doesn't at first appeal to me – it just shows that South has some scattered values and owing to North's "phoney" club he doesn't know what else to do with them. Now West had a lovely time. Sometimes he bid his "spade suit" and the North–South contortions were wonderful to listen to before they finally rested in 4♠. 6♠ can, of course, be made.

On the second amusing hand the conventional 1♣ as applied by Terence Reese came good. West dealt at love all:

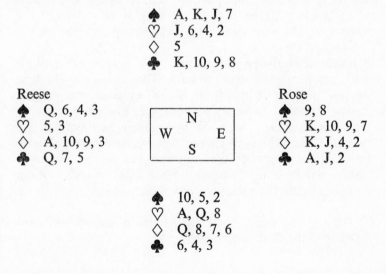

♠	A, K, J, 7
♡	J, 6, 4, 2
◇	5
♣	K, 10, 9, 8

Reese
♠ Q, 6, 4, 3
♡ 5, 3
◇ A, 10, 9, 3
♣ Q, 7, 5

Rose
♠ 9, 8
♡ K, 10, 9, 7
◇ K, J, 4, 2
♣ A, J, 2

♠ 10, 5, 2
♡ A, Q, 8
◇ Q, 8, 7, 6
♣ 6, 4, 3

Terence, sitting West, elected to open with 1♣, a bid which in his adaptation of the Precision Club (out of Little Major by Mini No-trump?) showed either 16 or more points or a balanced hand of about 7 points. When East's response of 1NT was passed round to North he guessed which type it was! He bid 2♣. After two passes West doubled – he had a maximum weak 1♣, after all. North and East passed and South essayed 2♢, West doubled again to show his extra 10 and North SOS-redoubled. His stiff upper lip trembling a little, South took himself out to 2♡ – and yet again a double. In a voice consigning the mini-club to perdition South settled for 2♠ and Terence, possibly because he held a fourth trump in addition to his 8 points and a 10, doubled firmly. After all this South ended with seven tricks and minus 100 points.

BLUE TEAM V. SHARIF CIRCUS

Promotion of bridge events has been growing steadily in many countries. In Britain we have been waiting patiently, and only in recent years have we been lucky enough to find sponsors like Cutty Sark, Martell, Harper's Bazaar, the *Guardian* and other national newspapers for special events. This made it possible in January 1971 for the "Blue Team" – the unbeaten Italian world champions – to come in full strength to London to play at the Mayfair Theatre against the best British players. With Omar Sharif as their non-playing captain this had to be a great occasion. For me it was very nostalgic – perhaps there will never again be anything like the Blue Team. Their discipline, defence, card-play and judgment are impeccable; they are also (almost an unknown thing in top bridge circles) both charming and modest, criticising only their own performances.

Here is an example of Belladonna's immaculate card reading. East dealt at game all:

```
                    ♠  A, 9, 5, 3, 2
                    ♡  J, 8, 2
                    ◇  8
                    ♣  K, 10, 8, 2
♠  Q, 8              ┌─────────────┐         ♠  K, 10, 7, 6, 4
♡  A, 9, 5, 3        │      N      │         ♡  Q, 10, 6, 4
◇  J, 9, 3, 2        │  W       E  │         ◇  A, Q, 10, 5
♣  A, 7, 3           │      S      │         ♣  None
                    └─────────────┘
                    ♠  J
                    ♡  K, 7
                    ◇  K, 7, 6, 4
                    ♣  Q, J, 9, 6, 5, 4
```

The bidding went as follows:

East	South	West	North
1♠	NB	2◇	NB
2♡	NB	3♡	NB
4♡	NB	NB	NB

South led the jack of clubs and Belladonna had to decide on his plan of action at trick one; this is imperative if you want to rank among the top players. He played low from dummy, ruffed with a low trump and led the 4 of spades. South played the jack and dummy's queen was taken by North's ace. North returned the 8 of diamonds.

By now declarer had a fairly clear picture of the hand. South was marked with a singleton spade – which he had not led, so he seemed to be marked with a trump trick. North had not attempted to give his partner a spade ruff immediately, so his diamond was a singleton and he was trying to set up a cross-ruff! Declarer therefore put up the ace of diamonds and played the queen of hearts, and now the contract was un-beatable whether South covered or not. In the event he did cover and dummy won with the ace. A small club was ruffed in the closed hand and another trump led; the defence could now come to only one spade trick, one trump trick and the king of diamonds.

In the other room East opened 1♠, South bid 2♣ and West doubled. This was not one of those "responsive" doubles and to my way of thinking was the worst of all evils – a simple 2◇ would have passed the time of day. North, well pleased, passed and East also passed. One of my pet theories – that a void in trumps can be fatal for the defence against a low-level doubled contract – came home very strongly. Just one doubled vulnerable overtrick.

Here is another Blue Team hand which I still enjoy vicariously. In Room 1 Belladonna and Avarelli were sitting East–West:

```
                    ♠  10
                    ♡  A, J, 9, 6
                    ◇  A, K, J, 6, 5
                    ♣  8, 7, 6

♠ K, 9, 8, 6, 4, 3      ┌─────────┐      ♠  Q, 7, 2
♡ 8                     │    N    │      ♡  10, 5
◇ 4                     │ W     E │      ◇  Q, 10, 9, 3
♣ K, Q, 5, 3, 2         │    S    │      ♣  A, J, 9, 4
                        └─────────┘

                    ♠  A, J, 5
                    ♡  K, Q, 7, 4, 3, 2
                    ◇  8, 7, 2
                    ♣  10
```

The bidding:

East	South	West	North
NB	1♡	1♠	2♠
3♣	4♡	4♠	4NT
NB	5◇	5♠	NB
NB	Double	NB	NB
NB			

And North–South thought that this was the best they could do.

North led the king of diamonds and then, in view of his partner's 2, switched to hearts. Declarer ruffed the second round, and since the bidding indicated either the ace of trumps or a singleton with North, he correctly led towards the queen of trumps in dummy, thus limiting his losers to three tricks.

At the other table Pabis-Ticci and d'Alelio were North–South. Owing to the requirements of their system South passed and West opened with a weak 2♠. Here is the full bidding sequence:

East	South	West	North
NB	NB	2♠	Double
3♠	4♠	NB	5♡
5♣	6♡	NB	NB
Double	NB	NB	NB

North's double of 2♠ was informatory.

Pabis-Ticci, North, won the opening spade lead in dummy, ruffed a spade, crossed to dummy with the queen of trumps and ruffed his last spade with the ace of trumps. He then played his last trump from hand, overtaking in dummy, and rattled off the rest. West discarded all his spades, his singleton diamond and the 5 of clubs. Pabis-Ticci discarded from his hand a low diamond and his three clubs and East left himself with ♢ Q, 10, 3 and the ace of clubs. Declarer now popped East in with the ace of clubs for a forced lead to his ♢ A, K, J.

East–West were not overjoyed with their defence, but that's the sort of thing that happens against a team who rarely make mistakes.

Of course no think-back would be complete without a memory or two of the handsome Omar Sharif and his Bridge Circus. Mr Sharif calls it his circus because (whenever filming allows) the team travels around having lots of fun and playing a lot of good bridge. When his team-mates play foolishly (would you believe?) he calls them his "animals". They play the latest version of one of the club systems and they all assure me that it is easy to learn and wonderful to play: I have yet to be convinced. The following hand, for instance, is not so much a system but more a play of life. North dealt at game all:

♠ A, Q
♥ A, K, 10, 8, 7
♦ K, 4
♣ J, 7, 5, 3

♠ 8, 4
♥ 9, 6
♦ A, J, 6, 5
♣ Q, 9, 8, 6, 4

```
        N
    W       E
        S
```

♠ 10, 7, 6, 3, 2
♥ Q, J, 4
♦ Q, 10
♣ A, 10, 2

♠ K, J, 9, 5
♥ 5, 3, 2
♦ 9, 8, 7, 3, 2
♣ K

This was the Circus bidding:

North	East	South	West
1♣[1]	NB	1♥[2]	NB
2♥[3]	NB	3♥[4]	NB
4♥[5]	NB	NB	NB

[1] A strong hand, forcing for at least one round.
[2] Showing 7 points minimum.
[3] Long suit and looking for more information.
[4] South's distribution justifies this further effort.
[5] North hopes that the hands fit and bids game.

West led the 9 of clubs against Omar Sharif's contract of 4♥. East won with the ace and returned the 2, which declarer ruffed. He then led a spade to the ace and ruffed another club. After two rounds of trumps he overtook the queen of spades with the king and discarded his last club on the jack of spades. Disappointingly the 10 of spades failed to drop and he had to rely on the position of the ace of diamonds. He had given himself as many chances as possible and deserved his success.

THE *Guardian* EASTER TOURNAMENT

No other British open event attracts more overseas visitors than the *Guardian* Easter Tournament; there is always a representative sprinkling of the world's best players. The competitions take place in the comfortable, pleasant surroundings of the Europa Hotel in London, where the post-mortems go on far into the night in the lounges. Great interest is added by Viewgraph, a sort of television set-up where people can watch the hands that have been played. A panel of experts is in attendance to analyse and discuss the various bids and plays. The following hand caused great commotion. It was dealt by South at game to East–West:

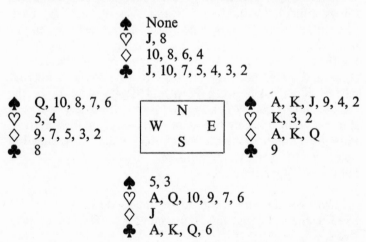

```
                    ♠ None
                    ♡ J, 8
                    ◇ 10, 8, 6, 4
                    ♣ J, 10, 7, 5, 4, 3, 2

♠ Q, 10, 8, 7, 6          N          ♠ A, K, J, 9, 4, 2
♡ 5, 4                               ♡ K, 3, 2
◇ 9, 7, 5, 3, 2     W         E      ◇ A, K, Q
♣ 8                      S           ♣ 9

                    ♠ 5, 3
                    ♡ A, Q, 10, 9, 7, 6
                    ◇ J
                    ♣ A, K, Q, 6
```

At most tables South opened the bidding with 1♡, West and North passed and then the fun began. Best results were

obtained by East when he bid 4♠ immediately and North–
South pusillanimously allowed him to play there. Some
Norths, after 4♠ from East and passes from South and
West, bid an "Unusual" 4NT (asking partner to bid his best
minor) and struck gold when South responded with 5♣.
Some Norths were doubled after being pushed into 6♣ and,
of course, made it. Prince Waldeck and Dr Chodziesner
were pushed to 7♣. East obligingly led the ace of spades,
and with the help of the heart finesse all thirteen tricks came
rolling home.

Louis Tarlo and Leon Tintner had to laugh about their
misfortune. Against them a LOL (i.e. Little Old Lady,
which is a euphemism for the sort of opponent, of any age or
sex, who gives the experts trouble because no one at the
table has any idea what is going on) opened 2♡ – a bid I
wouldn't criticise severely on South's attractive distribution.
This was passed to East, who bid 4♣; but the LOL had
not yet shown her all. She bid 5♣, which was raised to a
confident 6♣ by her partner.

The most amusing result came when South opened 1♡,
West and North passed and East bid 2♡. South tried to make
things difficult by bidding 4♡ and West called 4♠. East,
dazzled by his 20 points and wishing to protect his king of
hearts from the opening lead, found the "master" bid of 6NT.
South doubled and, trustingly, West passed (remember
clubs had never been mentioned). But I should think that
partnership trust between West and East will never be the
same again. It can't often happen that a vulnerable partnership plays in a freely-bid slam and never makes a trick.
Poor West followed the play as though watching a Wimbledon
final – his head weaving from side to side as trick after trick
fell to the opposition.

Baron von Dewitz is ever an optimist. He likes to bid his
hand to the full – and this South hand was fuller than many
I've seen him bid!

South dealt at game to East–West:

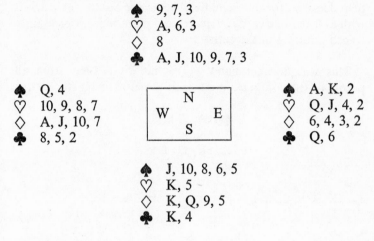

```
                    ♠  9, 7, 3
                    ♡  A, 6, 3
                    ◇  8
                    ♣  A, J, 10, 9, 7, 3

♠  Q, 4                    N              ♠  A, K, 2
♡  10, 9, 8, 7      W           E         ♡  Q, J, 4, 2
◇  A, J, 10, 7            S               ◇  6, 4, 3, 2
♣  8, 5, 2                                ♣  Q, 6

                    ♠  J, 10, 8, 6, 5
                    ♡  K, 5
                    ◇  K, Q, 9, 5
                    ♣  K, 4
```

The bidding:

South	West	North	East
1♠	NB	2♣	NB
2◇	NB	4♠	NB
NB	NB		

Although it is generally good policy to bid close games at teams-of-four scoring, North should have taken into account the fact that he had no fit in either of his partner's suits. He should have bid only 3♠; then South, with a poor trump suit and no aces, would have passed. As it was, however, Baron von Dewitz had to prove the partnership's pudding in the play.

West led the 10 of hearts, which declarer won in hand with the king. He played two rounds of clubs, and when East dropped the queen on the second round, he led the jack from dummy. East ruffed low to kill a winner, but declarer overruffed and then made his contract by playing two rounds of trumps. His opponents made only two trump tricks and the ace of diamonds.

It is hard to blame East for ruffing low, but had he been more alert he would have known that one discard could not help declarer, for on the bidding sequence South was marked with at least nine cards in spades and diamonds. A pleasantly spiced pudding in the eating!

This was another hand where the winds blew from all points of the compass. West dealt at game to North–South:

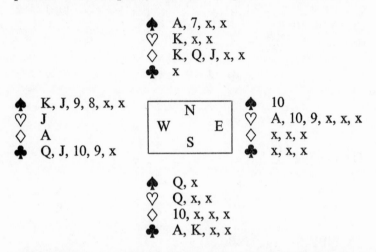

♠ A, 7, x, x
♡ K, x, x
◇ K, Q, J, x, x
♣ x

♠ K, J, 9, 8, x, x
♡ J
◇ A
♣ Q, J, 10, 9, x

♠ 10
♡ A, 10, 9, x, x, x
◇ x, x, x
♣ x, x, x

♠ Q, x
♡ Q, x, x
◇ 10, x, x, x
♣ A, K, x, x

Varying contracts in all four suits were played; the most popular was 3♠ doubled, played by West. Where the defence kicked off with diamonds and declarer was forced at every opportunity, the hand became unmanageable. When North started with his singleton club he got his ruff all right, but by guessing the trump situation correctly declarer made his nine tricks.

At John Collings's table – and we all know John – the wind rose to gale force. This was the "lovely biddings":

West	North	East	South
1♠	2◇	NB	3◇
3♠	Double	NB	3NT
Double	Redouble	NB	NB
NB			

John, sitting South, decided to try for a vulnerable game rather than take a non-vulnerable penalty. He may have had a moment of regret when dummy went down, but at match-pointed pairs, doubled and redoubled, he had to make the contract or settle for what is known on such occasions as bottom result.

West led the queen of clubs, which was allowed to hold. He continued with the jack of clubs. Declarer won with the king and continued with a diamond to West's singleton ace. West carried on with clubs. Declarer won with the ace and followed with a diamond to dummy.

John now tried to assess the situation. It seemed that West must have at least a six-card suit for his rebid of spades at the three level. East had not petered to show interest in clubs, so it seemed that West had five of them. He had shown up with a singleton diamond and therefore he could not have more than one heart. If his singleton heart was the ace nothing could be done, so declarer had to assume that East held that card.

Declarer cashed one more round of diamonds and led a low heart from dummy towards his Q, x, x. East could not afford to go in with the ace, for that would have given the ninth trick, so he played low.

When West's jack fell under the queen of hearts, John, secure in his analysis, led a club and West was end-played: he had to lead from his king of spades. You can see that declarer had to bank on his judgment and discard hearts from both dummy and his own hand on West's club winners.

Readers might observe that an imaginative lead of the singleton jack of hearts would have destroyed any chance of making the contract.

September
Morocco

The first international bridge festival in Morocco was organised in 1969 by the Royal Moroccan Bridge Federation as part of the King's fortieth birthday celebrations. It is no exaggeration to say that the participants were royally received. The atmosphere, though often tense, was always cordial; the championships were smoothly organised by G. Tribel, ably assisted by José le Dentu of *Le Figaro*, and I was quite impressed by the general standard of the play. There were excellent players among our hosts, notably Sebti, Danan, Bohbot, Alami, the charming Mme Tuny Cohen, Ohayon and Amar.

The pairs championship lasted four days with 96 pairs competing. It was won by Avarelli and Belladonna (Italy), with Jais and Trezel (France) second, Yallouze and Gresh (France) third, and J. Cansino and I fourth – the only pair from Britain. Cruz and Calheiros from Portugal came fifth, and the next two places were taken by all-Moroccan partnerships. The teams event was won by four members of the Italian Blue Team – Belladonna, Avarelli, Pabis-Ticci and d'Alelio – with a young Moroccan team second.

My partner and I had a rather dramatic passage through the pairs event. On the first day we scored 66 per cent, on the second about 59 per cent, and on the third only 49 per cent, dropping from second to twelfth position. But our fourth session became the sensation of the day, for we scored over 72 per cent. Here is one of our lucky hands from this last session, when everything was going our way – which explains the optimistic contract. My partner, sitting South, opened 1♡ as dealer. I bid 2♣, partner said 2NT and I raised him to 3NT:

```
              ♠  A, 10
              ♡  2
              ◇  9, 7, 6, 5, 3
              ♣  K, Q, 9, 6, 5

♠  Q, 8, 6, 5        ┌──────────────┐      ♠  J, 7, 3, 2
♡  Q, J, 9, 8        │      N       │      ♡  10, 7, 3
◇  4, 2              │  W       E   │      ◇  K, Q, J, 10
♣  8, 4, 2           │      S       │      ♣  A, J
                     └──────────────┘
              ♠  K, 9, 4
              ♡  A, K, 6, 5, 4
              ◇  A, 8
              ♣  10, 7, 3
```

West led the 5 of spades. Dummy played the 10, East the jack and South considered the hand carefully before winning the trick with the king. It did not look as if it would help him to duck, and he needed the ace of spades in dummy as an entry. He had to make sure of four club tricks in order to make his contract, so at trick 2 he played the 10 of clubs. West played low, declarer played the queen in dummy, and East took the trick with the ace, returning the king of diamonds. Cansino played the ace of diamonds, led another club and hardly hesitated before playing the king in dummy, dropping East's jack.

He reasoned as follows. East would not have taken the ace of clubs if he had not held A, J or ace bare; and the latter did not seem likely, because with four clubs to the J, 8 West might have covered the 10. This logical card-reading was rewarded by a top score, because although a few other declarers made nine tricks (especially those who were playing from North's hand), we were the only pair to bid game and make it.

Francisco Calheiros, the president of the Portuguese Bridge Federation, and his partner, Joao Cruz, scored an excellent result against Jonathan Cansino and me on the hand below, dealt by South at game to East–West:

99

Cruz
- ♠ Q, 10, 8, 5, 4
- ♡ J, 8, 5, 3
- ◇ 9, 4
- ♣ 5, 4

Cansino
- ♠ K
- ♡ 7, 6, 2
- ◇ A, K, J, 8, 5, 3
- ♣ 8, 7, 6

```
      N
  W       E
      S
```

Markus
- ♠ J, 9, 3, 2
- ♡ K, 4
- ◇ Q, 10, 7, 6
- ♣ K, Q, 2

Calheiros
- ♠ A, 7, 6
- ♡ A, Q, 10, 9
- ◇ 2
- ♣ A, J, 10, 9, 3

Bidding:

South	West	North	East
1♣	1◇	NB	2NT
3♡	NB	4♡[1]	NB
NB	NB		

[1] Partner had shown a hand very strong in distribution or tricks, and two doubletons with four trumps should be useful; in any case a courageous bid.

West played two rounds of diamonds. Declarer ruffed the second and played the ace and then the jack of clubs. East took this last trick with the king and played the 2 of spades. Declarer played low and West took the trick with the king. At this stage, the defence had already taken three tricks and Cansino (West) decided that it could not cost anything, but might help, to lead another diamond. Declarer ruffed in dummy, as he could not afford to be shortened again in his own hand in case there were three trumps to the king in East's hand. He played a low heart, finessed successfully, ruffed a club with the jack of trumps, played the last trump from dummy and drew the remaining trump; so he made his contract for + 420 – a near top. (Some East–West pairs had lost 500, going two down doubled.) Cruz turned to Cansino and said gently "You could have beaten the contract." Of course we could; can you find the solution?

Cansino saw it very quickly. West leads the king of spades. Declarer cannot get in to finesse in hearts without first allowing East to take a club trick. East then gives her partner a spade ruff and West leads a small diamond (!) from A, K, J. East gets in with the queen and West makes one more ruff for one down.

As I keep on repeating, most contracts could be beaten if one only knew.

Here is a hand taken from the teams-of-four final, played at the Hilton Hotel in lovely Rabat and watched on Bridgerama by many spectators. South dealt at game to North–South:

```
                    ♠  A, Q, 10, 7, 6
                    ♡  A, J, 10
                    ◇  9
                    ♣  A, J, 8, 7

♠  K, J, 5, 4            ┌─────────┐         ♠  9, 8, 3
♡  6, 2                  │    N    │         ♡  K, Q, 8, 5
◇  Q, 10, 8, 7, 6, 4, 3 │ W     E │         ◇  A, 2
♣  None                 │    S    │         ♣  10, 9, 5, 3
                        └─────────┘
                    ♠  2
                    ♡  9, 7, 4, 3
                    ◇  K, J, 5
                    ♣  K, Q, 6, 4, 2
```

The young Rabat East–West pair sacrificed with 4◇ against what appeared to be a cast-iron 3NT bid by the Italian North–South pair, and they lost 500 points. As the Bridgerama commentator remarked, this seemed to be a good result. Hearing this on my headphones I reported to the astonished commentator the following events in the closed room.

The Rabat North–South pair reached 3NT after Bella-donna, playing with Avarelli, had intervened as West with 2◊. West led the 6 of hearts, declarer played the 10 from dummy, East took the trick with the queen and immediately switched to a low diamond. Declarer played the jack, West won with the queen and led another heart. South thought he was in desperate straits; he felt he could not allow East to get in and lead another diamond, and it seemed obvious that West had led from a short heart suit. If he could prevent East from taking another trick he might come to his ninth trick by forcing West to play away from his (presumed) ace of diamonds. He therefore went up with the ace of hearts and rattled off his club winners, producing the following result:

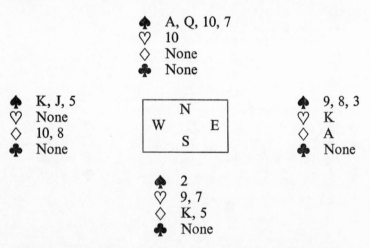

He then finessed the queen of spades, cashed the ace, and played a third round of spades, hopefully throwing the lead to West with the king. Imagine his horror when West continued with a low diamond to his partner's ace and the king of hearts provided the setting trick.

Here is a hand skilfully played by Leon Yallouze when he and Michel Lebel narrowly failed to win a Moroccan Tournament. East dealt at game to North–South:

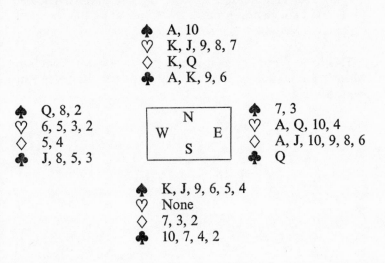

♠ A, 10
♡ K, J, 9, 8, 7
♢ K, Q
♣ A, K, 9, 6

♠ Q, 8, 2
♡ 6, 5, 3, 2
♢ 5, 4
♣ J, 8, 5, 3

N
W   E
S

♠ 7, 3
♡ A, Q, 10, 4
♢ A, J, 10, 9, 8, 6
♣ Q

♠ K, J, 9, 6, 5, 4
♡ None
♢ 7, 3, 2
♣ 10, 7, 4, 2

Bidding:

East	South	West	North
1♢	1♠	NB	2♢
3♢	3♠	NB	4♠
NB	NB	NB	

Declarer realised that he had to make use of the heart suit and he seemed to have enough entry cards. He could see a diamond loser, a possible trump loser and a possible club loser. He placed East with six diamonds and at least two honours in hearts, or one honour plus the queen of trumps.

East took the ace of diamonds and returned a diamond. Declarer led the 9 of hearts from dummy, East played the 10 and declarer ruffed. He then played a trump and guessed right, taking the trick with the 10. On the 8 of hearts East played low and declarer discarded a diamond. He then played another heart and ruffed, entered dummy with the ace of trumps, played the king of clubs, ruffed the fourth round of hearts, drew West's queen of trumps and finessed safely against West's jack of clubs.

I say "safely" because by then he had counted ten red cards and two spades in East's hand: therefore the queen of clubs must have been bare. Well played Leon!

This hand produced an interesting post-mortem dissection when Toni Trad was declarer, sitting South. East dealt at game all:

```
              ♠  5, 4, 3
              ♡  Q, 8, 2
              ◇  A, 10, 8, 6, 4, 3
              ♣  8

♠  6, 2                       ♠  K, Q, 9, 8, 7
♡  J, 10, 7, 5, 3      N      ♡  A, 9
◇  5, 2            W       E  ◇  Q, 9, 7
♣  10, 5, 4, 2        S      ♣  K, Q, 3

              ♠  A, J, 10
              ♡  K, 6, 4
              ◇  K, J
              ♣  A, J, 9, 7, 6
```

The bidding:

East	South	West	North
1♠	1NT	NB	3NT
NB	NB	NB	

West led the 5 of hearts, dummy played low and East correctly inserted the 9, won by declarer's king. South now found the good shot of the jack of diamonds. Had West covered with the queen he would have ducked in dummy, but as things were the jack rode round to East, who made a big mistake by winning with the queen.

The only hope for the defence now seemed to be that West held ♣ J, x, x, x, so East switched to the king of clubs. Declarer ducked but took the continuation of the queen with the ace and cashed the jack. The king of diamonds came next, overtaken by the ace, and when the diamonds behaved South was home. In fact he made an overtrick by guessing the heart position.

The post-mortem centred the blame on East for not ducking the jack of diamonds at trick two. But Toni Trad immediately found the answer: "I would have made it by playing East for doubleton ace of hearts." "True. But suppose West had led his partner's suit? Now the contract can always be defeated if East ducks the jack of diamonds." "Oh, no," said Toni, "I have to play off the diamond king and the heart king, and when East ducks, once again play him for the doubleton ace of hearts." "True. But suppose East wins the diamond jack with the queen and clears the spades?" "Then when I rattle the diamonds he is in trouble for discards and I must make two heart or two club tricks."

Michel Lebel is a most impressive player. He was sitting South on the hand below, dealt by North at game all:

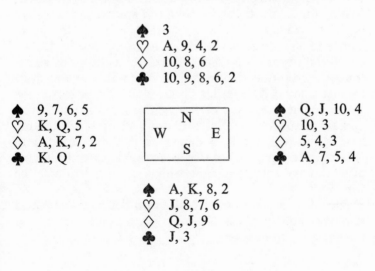

```
              ♠ 3
              ♡ A, 9, 4, 2
              ◇ 10, 8, 6
              ♣ 10, 9, 8, 6, 2

♠ 9, 7, 6, 5         N           ♠ Q, J, 10, 4
♡ K, Q, 5      W           E     ♡ 10, 3
◇ A, K, 7, 2         S           ◇ 5, 4, 3
♣ K, Q                           ♣ A, 7, 5, 4

              ♠ A, K, 8, 2
              ♡ J, 8, 7, 6
              ◇ Q, J, 9
              ♣ J, 3
```

The bidding:

North	East	South	West
NB	NB	1♠	Double
1NT	Double	NB	NB
2♣	Double	2♡	Double
NB	NB	NB	

You may disapprove of this sequence but it is not untypical of the scratching about for match-points to which one has to resort in pairs events – everybody hunting tops.

West did all he could to help Lebel by leading the A, K of diamonds, on which declarer carefully discarded the Q, J (being short of entries to dummy). He then continued to aid declarer by cashing the K, Q of clubs and finally putting declarer on table with the 10 of diamonds.

Declarer now found a classic way of coping with the trump suit. He could place West with ♡ K, Q on the bidding, and to avoid losing two tricks in the suit he had to "pin" East's hoped-for 10. He led the 2 of hearts from table, and when East followed with the 3 he played the 6 from his own hand. West won with the queen and again missed his chance of beating the contract. The fear of a ruff and discard, always a bogey to players who do not bother to count the hand, reared its ugly head, so he chose to play a spade. In fact a ruff and discard is a killer for declarer as he needs all his trumps for a further finesse against West's K, x and to draw the last trump before setting up the clubs. Declarer won the spade and led the jack of hearts, West refused to cover, dummy played low and East's 10 dropped. West's last trump was drawn with the 9 in dummy and clubs played until East covered with the ace. Declarer ruffed, cashed the king of spades and entered dummy with a spade ruff to cash the winning club.

Thus does a good player cash in on defender's muddled thinking. You should double only when your defence is at least as good as declarer's play.

At our table the bidding was different. South did not bid until we had reached 4♠; then he came to life and doubled. My partner, Toni Trad, was declarer sitting West and we too had our share of help from the defence. North led the ace of hearts and then switched to a diamond. Trad cashed the K, Q of hearts, discarding a diamond from dummy, and then the K, Q of clubs followed by the 5 of trumps. South won with the king and played the queen of diamonds, taken by West, and this was the position:

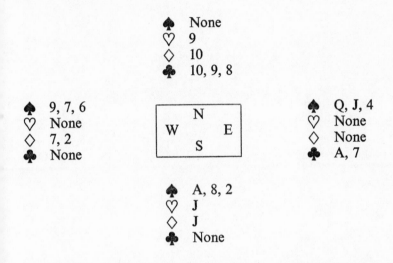

```
                    ♠  None
                    ♡  9
                    ◇  10
                    ♣  10, 9, 8

♠  9, 7, 6            ┌─────────┐         ♠  Q, J, 4
♡  None              │    N    │         ♡  None
◇  7, 2           W  │         │  E      ◇  None
♣  None              │    S    │         ♣  A, 7
                    └─────────┘

                    ♠  A, 8, 2
                    ♡  J
                    ◇  J
                    ♣  None
```

Declarer now ruffed a diamond with the jack of trumps and played the ace of clubs. South could make nothing but the ace of trumps.

Since that first visit I have returned to Morocco three times. It is not easy to explain why I find the country so fascinating. If you have never been to Morocco you can hardly imagine the kind of hospitality you can expect there. Luxury hotels, wonderful sight-seeing and exciting bridge are the order of the day. Some of the foreign players reckon they are nobbled by the lavish entertainment (not excluding the dancing girls); certainly it seems quite a struggle for foreign bridge-players to win there. I was quite thrilled when I was invited in December 1970 to participate in the Mixed Championship at Casablanca; my host and partner was David Amar. After all I had never played with him before and the field was strong; over 100 pairs competed.

Freak hands are always a guessing game, but David Amar and I came out on the right side on this one. East dealt at game to North–South:

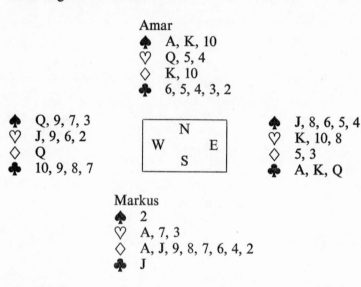

Amar
- ♠ A, K, 10
- ♡ Q, 5, 4
- ♢ K, 10
- ♣ 6, 5, 4, 3, 2

West:
- ♠ Q, 9, 7, 3
- ♡ J, 9, 6, 2
- ♢ Q
- ♣ 10, 9, 8, 7

East:
- ♠ J, 8, 6, 5, 4
- ♡ K, 10, 8
- ♢ 5, 3
- ♣ A, K, Q

Markus
- ♠ 2
- ♡ A, 7, 3
- ♢ A, J, 9, 8, 7, 6, 4, 2
- ♣ J

The bidding:

East	South	West	North
1♠	3♢	3♠	5♢
5♣	6♢	NB	NB
Double	NB	NB	NB

West led the 3 of spades, taken in dummy with the king. When West played the queen of diamonds on the trump lead declarer decided to place East with the king of hearts in view of the opening bid. He followed with the 10 of trumps and then the ace of spades, discarding a low heart. A spade was ruffed in hand and the trumps were cashed.

The position before the last diamond was played was:

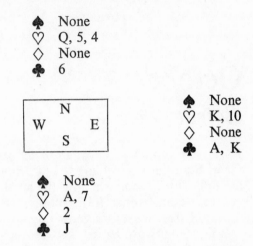

```
              ♠  None
              ♡  Q, 5, 4
              ◇  None
              ♣  6

Immaterial      ┌──────────────┐      ♠  None
                │      N       │      ♡  K, 10
                │  W       E   │      ◇  None
                │      S       │      ♣  A, K
                └──────────────┘

              ♠  None
              ♡  A, 7
              ◇  2
              ♣  J
```

Now came the *coup de grâce*. Declarer played his last trump, discarding dummy's club. East tried bravely by discarding the ace of clubs but David ignored this attempt and threw him in with the jack of clubs to the king. Poor East had now to lead away from the king of hearts into dummy's queen and declarer's ace.

It will be seen that if declarer had discarded his losing club on the king of spades he would have had no chance, for the defence must then come to two heart tricks.

October
Beirut

Beirut, the capital of Lebanon, is an exciting city, famous for its beautiful scenery and full of people who enjoy life to the full. There is something in the air that makes you gay: you take home wonderful memories and you make friends for life. I shall always long to go back.

Bridge events can be tedious – but not in Beirut, because after the bridge sessions the real fun begins: music, dancing, the wonderful show at the Casino and parties in people's homes where you are received with open arms. It is a strange, intoxicating mixture of Oriental splendour and Western influence, of zest for life and joy and laughter.

It was when our John Collings went to play in a tournament in Lebanon that he fell in love with his beautiful Noura – and what a handsome couple they make. (Yes, this too can happen when you take part in bridge tournaments.) I met Noura in Beirut long before John did, and she was the best mascot I ever had. That year I won the Mixed Pairs with Benito Garozzo and the Pairs with Fritzi Gordon, and my team – Fritzi Gordon, Nadine Ansay, Annie Pouldjian and I – were leading in the Teams of Four until the last round; then Noura was detained, so we had to be content with second place. First were Benito Garozzo, Omar Sharif, Leon Yallouze and George Gresh.

The Lebanese chess champion, Charlie Salameh, is a brilliant rubber-bridge player. He also plays in tournaments, but while waiting for the results he gets three players and talks them into playing his favourite game – money bridge. Here is an example of his cunning. His partner was the beautiful Sonya Gresh from Beirut. West was none other than the famous Mimmo d'Alelio of the Blue Team, partnered by one of the leading Lebanese lady players, Olga Menasseh.

West dealt at game all:

Salameh
♠ x, x
♡ None
◇ K, 10, 9, x, x, x, x
♣ A, x, x, x

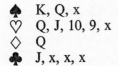
♠ K, Q, x
♡ Q, J, 10, 9, x
◇ Q
♣ J, x, x, x

♠ 10, 9, x, x
♡ K, x, x, x
◇ x
♣ K, Q, x, x

Mrs Gresh
♠ A, J, x, x
♡ A, x, x, x
◇ A, J, x, x
♣ x

The bidding went:

West	North	East	South
NB	NB	NB	1◇
1♡	2◇(!)	2♡	NB
NB	3◇	3♡	NB
NB	4◇	NB	NB
4♡	5◇	Double	NB
5♡	6◇	6♡	NB
NB	7◇	NB	NB
NB			

111

7◇ made. When I asked Charlie why he had bid only 2◇ he replied "I did not know how expensive 6♡ would be, or even 7, so I went slowly."

Here are two hands played in Beirut which illustrate what. I mean when I say that good judgment, bold decisions and logical thinking are all factors which contribute to successes.

In the first example my partner was Erwin Strauss, the son of the late Oscar Strauss, the composer, and an excellent musician and bridge player. He opened 1♣ and I heard a double on my right. (We were playing a natural system and not a short or prepared club.) I held ♠ 10, 6, 2; ♡ Q, 6, 5; ◇ Q, 7; ♣ A, K, 9, 4, 2. With very little defence in the major suits I jumped to 3NT: I could not think of any other bid. Everybody passed, West led the 3 of spades and I made 10 tricks for 430. Our team-mates were very pleased because their opponents had played in 3♣.

These were the four hands, dealt by North at love all:

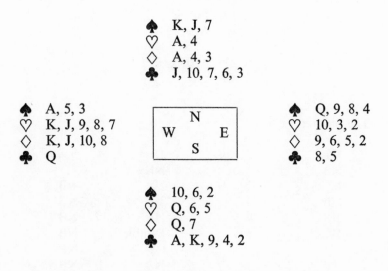

```
                    ♠ K, J, 7
                    ♡ A, 4
                    ◇ A, 4, 3
                    ♣ J, 10, 7, 6, 3

♠ A, 5, 3                N               ♠ Q, 9, 8, 4
♡ K, J, 9, 8, 7     W         E          ♡ 10, 3, 2
◇ K, J, 10, 8            S               ◇ 9, 6, 5, 2
♣ Q                                      ♣ 8, 5

                    ♠ 10, 6, 2
                    ♡ Q, 6, 5
                    ◇ Q, 7
                    ♣ A, K, 9, 4, 2
```

Then I watched Omar Sharif, who went ahead to win the Individual.

This hand helped:

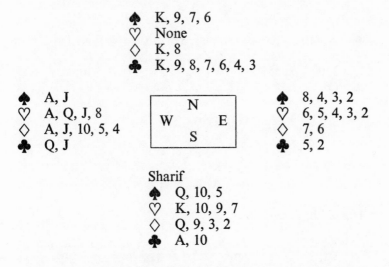

♠ K, 9, 7, 6
♡ None
◇ K, 8
♣ K, 9, 8, 7, 6, 4, 3

♠ A, J
♡ A, Q, J, 8
◇ A, J, 10, 5, 4
♣ Q, J

♠ 8, 4, 3, 2
♡ 6, 5, 4, 3, 2
◇ 7, 6
♣ 5, 2

Sharif
♠ Q, 10, 5
♡ K, 10, 9, 7
◇ Q, 9, 3, 2
♣ A, 10

West opened 2NT and North came in with 3♣. Since North–South were vulnerable, North was marked with a very long suit, as he was bidding it without two honours. When you own a long suit points become meaningless, so Sharif bid 3NT.

West doubled and led the jack of diamonds, won by dummy's king. Declarer then played a low club towards his ace and a small spade towards dummy's king. All West could do was to cash his three tricks and Omar scored 950 for a clear top.

Here is a classic example from the Lebanon Festival of Garozzo's technique in dummy play. West dealt at game to North–South:

113

Yallouze
- ♠ x, x
- ♡ 7, x, x
- ◇ A, Q, x, x
- ♣ 10, 8, x, x

♠ A, Q, x, x, x   ♠ K, J, 10, x, x
♡ 6   ♡ K, Q, J, 9
◇ J, 9, 8, x, x, x   ◇ 10, x
♣ Q   ♣ 9, x

```
        N
    W       E
        S
```

Garozzo
- ♠ x
- ♡ A, 10, 8, x, x
- ◇ K
- ♣ A, K, J, 7, x, x

The bidding:

West	North	East	South
NB	NB	1♠	2♡
4♠	NB	NB	5♣
NB	NB	NB	

Opposite a passed partner South had a difficult bidding problem. If he doubled 1♠ partner might be tempted to try 5◇ over a bid of 4♠ by West, and then he (South) would have to look for a fit on a very high level. For this reason he preferred to bid both his suits. He mentioned hearts first because in a pairs event a heart contract produces a higher score and a better result.

West led the ace of spades and East played the jack. This could have meant either that East wanted a continuation of spades or that he had some strength in hearts. In any case from West's point of view the best chance was to find partner with the ace of hearts. If partner had desired a diamond switch he would have played a low spade. (The old myth that there is no such thing as a "McKenney" on the first trick was exploded some time ago.)

114

Garozzo won the heart lead with the ace, drew one round of trumps, cashed his king of diamonds and entered dummy with the 10 of clubs. He then ruffed a spade with a low trump and entered dummy again with the 8 of clubs. He discarded two of his hearts on the two master diamonds and another on the fourth diamond. West had to take this trick and was forced to present declarer with a ruff and discard of his last heart loser. In fact, declarer played the hand for the only chance, namely a 6–5–1–1 distribution in West, which was an exact replica of his own pattern.

At some tables East–West played in 4♠ doubled for one down. Only one declarer was allowed to make 4♠. In this case, after the defenders had cashed the ace of clubs and ace of hearts and exited with a trump, East stripped her hand of hearts and clubs, finishing in dummy. She then led a low diamond; North played low and South took the trick with the king. Whatever South returned East could trump in dummy and get rid of her second diamond loser.

This was a blatant example of careless defence. North had no reason for playing low. He could not gain by not playing the ace of diamonds.

November
The Algarve

The Algarve Tournament has become one of my favourite events. It offers the most beautiful scenery, an ideal climate, excellent hotel accommodation and wonderful golf courses. The great golf champion Henry Cotton resides there. In the evenings there is entertainment in the night club of the Hotel Alvor Praia, where the tournament is held. Every night you can join in different kinds of fun, such as dancing competitions, fancy-dress parties (with juries awarding prizes for the best competitors), folk-singing and so on.

In the afternoons the bridge competitors assemble – some of them very strong players, and others who take part because they enjoy meeting the famous and get a special thrill from scoring well against the experts.

In 1970 Francisco Calheiros, the president of the Portuguese Bridge Federation, acted as compère during our night-club sessions and the dance floor was taken over by the bridge players. Giorgio Belladonna won all the bridge events (needless to say), but he also won the prize for the best individual dancing performance, and to everybody's surprise

116

(and my joy) I was among those who qualified for the final of the Cha-Cha-Cha and the Valse, partnered by a charming Portuguese. This was my greatest success.

My only triumph at the bridge table was in the team event; my team qualified in front of the Italian team (the eventual winners). The hand below, dealt by West, was the first in this event. My partner was Calheiros, sitting South, and it was the first time we had played together:

```
                    ♠  None
                    ♡  J, 8, 7, 5, 3
                    ◇  K, 9, 4, 2
                    ♣  A, 7, 5, 3

♠  J, 9, 8, 5          ┌──────────┐        ♠  K, 6, 4, 3
♡  6, 2               │    N     │        ♡  Q, 9, 4
◇  A, Q, 10, 8, 3     │ W     E  │        ◇  J, 7, 6, 5
♣  10, 6              │    S     │        ♣  K, 2
                      └──────────┘
                    ♠  A, Q, 10, 7, 2
                    ♡  A, K, 10
                    ◇  None
                    ♣  Q, J, 9, 8, 4
```

The bidding went very smoothly:

West	North	East	South
NB	NB	NB	1♣
NB	1♡	NB	1♠
NB	2◇[1]	NB	3♠
NB	5♣	NB	6♣
NB	NB	NB	

[1] A test for a new partnership. I wanted to find out more about his hand and at the same time to convey a picture of my own.

117

We were both very pleased that we managed to reach this perfect slam contract on comparatively meagre values. As you can see, there is no lead by West that can beat it. If West leads a trump, declarer is forced to take the heart finesse, which succeeds. But as Calheiros got the ace of diamonds led, he tried to make his contract without taking the heart finesse. He ruffed the ace of diamonds and played first the king of hearts and then the queen of trumps. If the trump finesse had worked he could safely have surrendered a heart trick. In the event, it did not, so he could not. East took the queen of trumps with the king and played a low diamond. Declarer ruffed, cashed the jack of trumps and then the ace of hearts, ruffed a spade in dummy, discarded the losing 10 of hearts on the king of diamonds, ruffed a heart and so came to 12 tricks.

As we had five players in our team, I decided to make a most necessary visit to the hairdresser and was convinced that my team would safely reach the final without my help. But to my great disappointment they were beaten by Gresh's French team in a short match of 16 boards. There was one decisive board which should have produced a swing of 26 IMPs in our favour.

What do you lead on ♠ 10, 9, x, x; ♡ 10, x; ♢ A, J, 10, x, x, x; ♣ x, when (after partner's opening bid of 3♠) you have succeeded in pushing opponents into 6♣? I was asked this question when I arrived after my team had finished the first eight boards. My reply was "The ace of diamonds, of course." "I wish you had been here," sighed my team-mate, "because we could have cashed two tricks in that suit."

Moral: If you push you must also know what to lead.

118

Here is a hand from an Algarve Pairs event which shows how effective the Italian systems are for slam bidding:

Delmouly
♠ x, x
♡ K, x
♢ K, Q, 9, x, x
♣ A, x, x, x

Sharif
♠ A, J, 10
♡ A, J, x
♢ A, x, x
♣ K, Q, J, x

Bidding (with no interference from East–West):

South	North
1♣	1NT
2♣	2♢
2NT	3♣
3♢	3♡
3♠	4♣
4♡	5NT
7♣	

Notes: 1♣ – A strong hand with upwards of 17 points.
1NT – Showing four "controls" (ace = two controls, king = one).
2♣ – Forcing.
2◇ – Natural.
2NT – Showing a 4–3–3–3 distribution.
3♣ – Natural.
3◇ – Natural.
3♡ – Cue bid, showing one of the kings.
3♠ – Cue bid.
4♣ – Cue bid.
4♡ – Cue bid.
5NT – Grand slam force, asking partner to bid 7♣ with two of the three top honours in that suit.

Jonathan Cansino and I bid as follows:

South	*North*
2NT	6NT

I could not bid 3◇ because we play a version of the Flint Convention, which says that when a 2NT opener hears 3◇ from partner he must bid 3♡ and thereafter hold his peace; so I settled for 6NT. As the diamond suit broke 2–3 and East held the queen of hearts, my partner automatically made thirteen tricks for a good score. But 7♣ is, of course, the par contract.

Here is an example of what I mean by good judgment. It occurred during a Pairs event at the Algarve Bridge Festival in 1969. Belladonna and Avarelli won the event in great style and my partner and I were satisfied with our result against them on the following hand.

North dealt at love all:

Belladonna
♠ A, K, Q, 8, 4, 2
♡ 5, 4, 2
◇ Q, 10, 6
♣ Q

Markus
♠ J, 5
♡ K, Q, J, 9, 8
◇ K, 7
♣ A, 10, 8, 3

```
      N
  W       E
      S
```

Cotter
♠ 9
♡ A, 10, 3
◇ 9, 4, 3
♣ K, J, 9, 7, 6, 5

Avarelli
♠ 10, 7, 6, 3
♡ 7, 6
◇ A, J, 8, 5, 2
♣ 4, 2

North	East	South	West
1♠	2♣	2♠	4♡[1]
4♠	5♡[2]	NB	NB
5♠[3]	NB	NB	Double[4]
NB	NB	NB	

[1] Instead of bidding 5♣ or 4♣ I chose 4♡. I wanted a heart lead against a spade contract and I still had time to bid 5♣ over 4♠.

[2] My partner made an excellent and courageous bid. He knew that he had meagre defence values against 4♠.

[3] North showed respect for our bidding and went to 5♠ –

[4] – which I doubled for two down.

You can see that if the ace of diamonds had been with North 4♠ would have been on, though 5♠ could not have been made; but 5♡ are unbeatable.

Judgment on a high level is something you can hardly learn. Experience helps, but I often say how lucky it was that I was born with a big nose and can often smell things.

There are hands which one cannot forget. Here is one of them. Jonathan Cansino was my partner at the Pairs Championship in the Algarve (1970). We played the first hand against a well-known Portuguese pair. This was the full hand and the bidding at love all, dealer West:

	♠ A, 10, 8, 7	
	♡ K, Q, 10, 4	
	◊ A, K, 8, 7, 6	
	♣ None	

♠ K, J		♠ Q, 9, 5, 3, 2
♡ A, J, 9, 3	N	♡ 2
◊ 2	W E	◊ Q, 5, 4
♣ A, K, Q, 10, 8, 7	S	♣ J, 9, 6, 5

	♠ 6, 4	
	♡ 8, 7, 6, 5	
	◊ J, 10, 9, 3	
	♣ 4, 3, 2	

The Bidding:

West	North	East	South
1♣	2♣	3♣	NB
3♡	NB[1]	3♠	NB
5♣	NB[2]	NB	5◊[3]
Double	NB	NB	NB

[1] Without a moment's hesitation Cansino passed.
[2] Again my partner passed without the slightest pause.
[3] I thought for a long time: and then I bid 5◊.

122

I made a bid of which I am not proud. I only tell this story to prove that I could never have bid 5◇ if my partner after his initial 2♣ overcall (a very strong bid indeed) had shown any further reaction to the subsequent bidding sequence. Cansino is one of the most ethical players and knows how to control his feelings. Most players in his position might have considered a further bid on his hand. I was puzzled because there was so much missing. As we have played very seldom together I wondered whether his pass could be interpreted as a forcing pass and as I could not double 5♣ I bid 5◇. The result was excellent for us, but I must repeat that I do not wish to boast of my decision to bid 5◇. When dummy went down I could hardly believe my eyes. Who else but Jonathan would have kept silent after 3♡ and 5♣ by West?

December
Spain

I have so far been only twice to Spain in spite of my zest for travel. I could not explain why. This does not mean that there are not very interesting bridge events in Spain; on the contrary many of my bridge friends have reported about the beautiful places, the perfect organisation and the wonderful hospitality they have enjoyed. I first went in November 1970, to Palma (Majorca), where we spent a wonderful week at the Melia–Bahia Palace.

The occasion of my second trip was an invitation to attend the 8th International Bridge Tournament at the Melia Don Pepe at Marbella–Malaga (11–18 December 1971) as the captain of a British team (T. Reese, M. Wolach, Mrs Gordon and myself), supported by Leon Yallouze. I am glad to be able to report that we won the team event – a victory that was made easier by the absence of the Blue Team, which was at that moment beating the Dallas Aces in Las Vegas. The Italian champions usually carry off the first prizes but one year (1967) Roger Trezel and José le Dentu won the Palma de Majorca pairs event with an incredible percentage of $66\frac{1}{2}$ over 4 sessions. Second were d'Alelio and Pabis-Ticci, third Avarelli and Belladonna and fourth Boender and Slavenburg from Holland.

Here is a nice hand from that occasion which gave the French pair one of their many tops. East dealt at love all:

R. Trezel
♠ 8, 4, 3
♡ A, K, 3
◇ K, 8, 2
♣ A, J, 7, 5

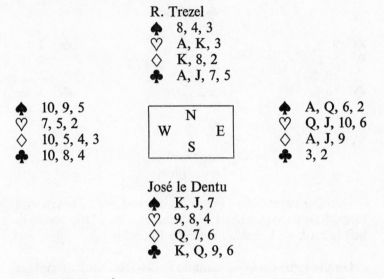

♠ 10, 9, 5
♡ 7, 5, 2
◇ 10, 5, 4, 3
♣ 10, 8, 4

♠ A, Q, 6, 2
♡ Q, J, 10, 6
◇ A, J, 9
♣ 3, 2

José le Dentu
♠ K, J, 7
♡ 9, 8, 4
◇ Q, 7, 6
♣ K, Q, 9, 6

The bidding:

East	South	West	North
1♡	NB	NB	Double
NB	2NT	NB	3NT
NB	NB	NB	

West led the 10 of spades and South was allowed to take the trick with the jack in his own hand. He entered dummy with a club and played a low diamond, winning the trick with the queen. He then entered dummy again with a club and played a spade. East took this trick and played the queen of hearts. Declarer won in dummy and cashed his last two club tricks, finishing in his own hand.

Here is the picture after two rounds of spades, one round of hearts, one round of diamonds and four rounds of clubs:

125

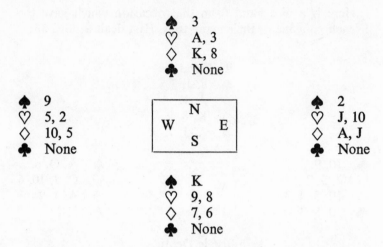

Declarer cashed the king of spades and ace of hearts and threw East in with a heart; East had had very little choice in her discards and declarer came to 10 tricks.

On the same occasion Camillo Pabis-Ticci took advantage of a favourable lead to make a slam which he and his partner, d'Alelio, reached. 6♣ seems an excellent contract, and the way these Italian champions play only a diamond lead could have beaten it:

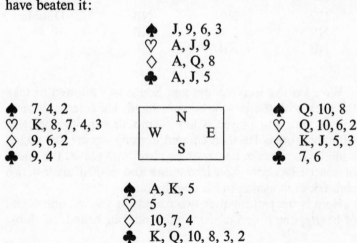

West chose the lead of the 7 of spades, declarer played the 9, East covered and declarer's king took the trick. He then carefully eliminated the heart suit by trumping both heart losers. He drew trumps, cashed the ace of spades and played a low spade. East had to take the trick with the queen and was faced with the unfortunate choice of two evils. He could play a diamond into dummy's tenace or a heart and thus give South a ruff and discard for one of his diamond losers. The second loser could be discarded on dummy's winning spade.

Here is the situation:

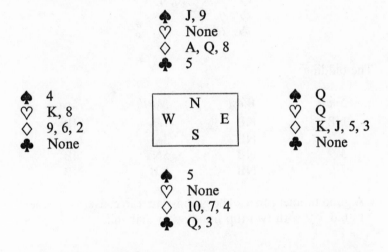

An amusing situation arose when Avarelli's son and Pabis-Ticci junior finished several places in front of Walter Avarelli senior and his partner, Paulo Frendo. The event was in the Festival at the Melia de la Costa del Sol in 1970, and the Pairs Championship was won by d'Alelio and Pabis-Ticci with two Spanish pairs, Munoz–Viedma and Alcala-Galvente, in second and third places.

A fascinating hand was played on this occasion by the Belgian player Verdonck in 7♡. South dealt at game to East–West:

```
              ♠  None
              ♡  K, 7, 2
              ◇  A, K, Q
              ♣  A, Q, 10, 9, 8, 7, 3
```

```
♠  A, 9, 6, 5, 3, 2          ┌─────────────┐          ♠  K, Q, 10, 7
♡  8                         │     N       │          ♡  J, 9, 6, 5
◇  10, 7, 4, 3               │  W     E    │          ◇  J, 8, 6
♣  K, 4                      │     S       │          ♣  J, 2
                             └─────────────┘
```

```
              ♠  J, 8, 4
              ♡  A, Q, 10, 4, 3
              ◇  9, 5, 2
              ♣  6, 5
```

The bidding:

South	West	North	East
NB	NB	1♣	NB
1♡	NB	3♣	NB
3♡	NB	5NT[1]	NB
7♡	NB	NB	NB

[1] A good moment to use the grand-slam force, asking partner to bid 7♡ with two top honours in that suit.

You may not approve of the final contract but you will agree with me that the Belgian declarer played it in masterly fashion.

West led the ace of spades. After ruffing and playing the king and a low trump, declarer learned the truth about the trump position and had to develop a plan to make 13 tricks in spite of it. He needed the club finesse plus a 2–2 break in that suit; 7♣ would have been much easier, but this was a pairs contest and 7♡ produced a better score. The main task for declarer here is to shorten his own hand in trumps after having finessed the clubs successfully. He had to perform what is known as a "Grand Coup". He played a third round of clubs, on which East discarded a diamond, and he ruffed with a low trump. He then entered dummy with a diamond and continued with the club suit:

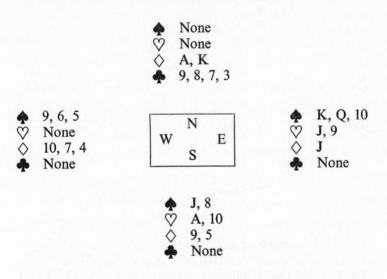

♠ None
♡ None
♢ A, K
♣ 9, 8, 7, 3

♠ 9, 6, 5
♡ None
♢ 10, 7, 4
♣ None

♠ K, Q, 10
♡ J, 9
♢ J
♣ None

♠ J, 8
♡ A, 10
♢ 9, 5
♣ None

If East ruffed declarer could overruff, draw the last trump and enter dummy to make the rest. If East refused to ruff he would discard all his spades and diamonds until the last two tricks when North held two winners in the minor suits, East J, 9 of trumps and declarer A, 10.

Again you can learn from this example that however complicated your task may seem to you, there is often a perfect way to reach your goal. Just try and visualise how the missing cards have to be placed and time it so that your opponents can do nothing about it. In fact you can often drive them into a position where they have to surrender or even help you actively to achieve your aim.

Here are two more hands which occurred in Spain. That old Vienna Coup keeps cropping up, sometimes by accident and sometimes by design, but there was no accidental play by d'Alelio on this hand. North dealt at love all:

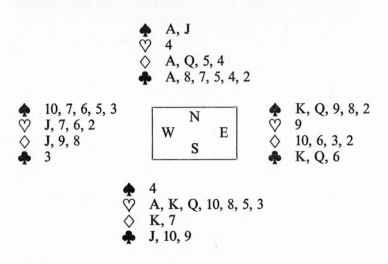

♠ A, J
♥ 4
♦ A, Q, 5, 4
♣ A, 8, 7, 5, 4, 2

♠ 10, 7, 6, 5, 3
♥ J, 7, 6, 2
♦ J, 9, 8
♣ 3

♠ K, Q, 9, 8, 2
♥ 9
♦ 10, 6, 3, 2
♣ K, Q, 6

♠ 4
♥ A, K, Q, 10, 8, 5, 3
♦ K, 7
♣ J, 10, 9

West led a spade against d'Alelio's contract of 6♡. Declarer won in dummy and played trumps. When West won the fourth round and continued with a spade, the only hope now seemed to be that one of the opponents held K, Q of clubs and four diamonds; so, in case that opponent was East, declarer executed a Vienna Coup by first cashing the ace of clubs, returning to his own hand with the king of diamonds and then running the hearts. On the last heart dummy could discard a club but East had to choose between ◇ 10, 6, 3 (against dummy's ◇ A, Q, 5) and ♣ K (against declarer's ♣ J, 10).

I heard that at another table the 3 of clubs was led against 6♡. Declarer could not, of course, risk an adverse ruff and there would be twelve top tricks if the hearts broke or the jack of hearts came down when they were first led. He therefore played the ace of clubs from dummy and followed

with trumps, West winning the fourth round. West now
switched to a spade, which declarer took with the ace. He
returned to his own hand with the king of diamonds and
played off his trumps. East had the impossible task of trying
to guard three suits – the king of spades and clubs and his
four diamonds – although the spade suit became immaterial
unless declarer held the 10 as well as the 4.

This hand was played by Belladonna. East–West game:

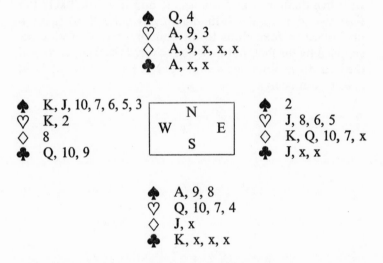

	♠	Q, 4
	♡	A, 9, 3
	◇	A, 9, x, x, x
	♣	A, x, x

♠	K, J, 10, 7, 6, 5, 3		♠	2
♡	K, 2		♡	J, 8, 6, 5
◇	8		◇	K, Q, 10, 7, x
♣	Q, 10, 9		♣	J, x, x

	♠	A, 9, 8
	♡	Q, 10, 7, 4
	◇	J, x
	♣	K, x, x, x

After West had originally passed and then intervened with
2♠, Belladonna (South) became declarer in a contract of
2NT. In pairs events +120 is generally a valuable score.
If North–South cannot make their no-trump contract, it
may be that East–West could have made +110 from 2♠.
Even if East–West fail in their contract by one trick, a score
of +100 is not likely to be a good score for North–South.

West led the jack of spades and dummy's queen took the
first trick. South played the 9 of hearts from dummy, East
covered with the jack, declarer with the queen and West

won with the king. West continued with the 10 of spades, on which East discarded a low club. Belladonna decided to wait in case the next trick could supply him with further information. West (a good player) was worried that he might squeeze his partner if he continued the spade suit, so he led the 8 of diamonds. South played low from dummy and East won with the queen and continued with the king of diamonds. Dummy took the trick with the ace and the king and ace of clubs were cashed. Declarer then played ace and another heart, finessing against East's ♡ Q, x. He had counted East with five diamonds and one spade and it was unlikely that East would keep the fifth diamond or the third heart in preference to four clubs to an honour. A further clue was supplied by the fact that East had covered the 9 of hearts with the jack; to an observant dummy player East was marked with J, 8, x, x in hearts.

For Further Reference

For the convenience of my readers, I am including some information about national and international bridge events and also the addresses of the bridge centres of those countries which stage attractive tournaments. It is quite possible that I have left some of them out, because it is a heavy task to collect all this information, but if I have inadvertently done so I hope to include them in the next edition of this book.

For detailed information and dates, conditions of entry, etc., of events in England write to:

> Mrs A. L. Fleming
> 12 Frant Road
> Tunbridge Wells
> Kent

Among the regular interesting events are:

January – EBU Spring Foursomes at the Grand Hotel, Eastbourne.
Guardian Easter Tournament – Europa Hotel, London.
London Congress – Berners Hotel, London. Late spring.
Yorkshire Congress – normally held at Scarborough in June.
August – EBU Summer Congress, Hotel Metropole, Brighton.
September – Somerset Congress and Kent Congress.
Autumn Congress – Grand Hotel, Eastbourne.
Harper's Bazaar Winter Tournament – December, at the Europa Hotel, London.

For events in Wales:

> Welsh Bridge Union
> (Mr C. E. A. Samuels)
> 220A Newport Road
> Cardiff
> Wales

will send you information about their programme. Events are often held at Porthcawl, which boasts a lovely golf course.

The Bridge Association of Yugoslavia organises several events in the most attractive resorts, and offers special terms for the participating bridge players. For details here you should write to:

> Fred Kulenovic
> President of the Technical Commission
> Yugoslav Bridge Federation
> Kuhaceva 13
> 41000 Zagreb
> Yugoslavia

A Spring Tournament is held usually in early May under the auspices of the Czech Bridge Association and the Town Council of Marienbad in Marienbad. I know the town very well from pre-war days, and I am sure that many bridge travellers would love this place and enjoy a trip there. For details write to:

> The Czech Bridge Association
> P.O. Box 1063
> Prague
> Czechoslovakia

The Northern Irish Bridge Union has already got the dates out for 1972. It holds a National Congress at Portrush from 20 to 27 September, and the Newcastle (Co. Down) Club holds an Open Congress early in June. There are, of course, other events held during the year, and for details of these write to:

> The Hon. Secretary
> NI Bridge Union
> Clovelly
> Sea Park
> Hollywood
> Co. Down

In Eire there are a lot of bridge activities but the dates for 1972 are uncertain. Congresses will be held at Tramore, Killarney and Sligo in May, and these events are especially attractive for bridge-playing golfers.

In Spain the most famous international festivals are the annual events at the Hotel Melia Don Pepe in Marbella in December, and in February at the Hotel Melia-Majorca (Palma de Majorca); in March at the Hotel Plaza (Madrid); and in April at the Hotel Calipolis (Sitges). Detailed information from:

> The Spanish Bridge Federation
> Travesera de las Cortes 63 al 71
> Barcelona 14
> Spain

Hungary offers its bridge players wonderful hospitality, excellent food and exciting bridge, and there you will meet players from those countries who cannot afford to send their teams to Western Europe. There is an international bridge festival on the shores of Lake Balaton in early June, and another in late autumn. For details of these write to:

> The Secretary General
> Budapesti Bridzs Egyesulet
> Postafiok 225
> Budapest 62
> Hungary

The Swiss Bridge Federation has become more and more active in recent years and the most important annual events are of course the International Bridge Week in St Moritz, usually held during the second half of January and lasting about 10 to 12 days, and the popular bridge week in Crans-sur-Sierre in mid-March. A combined French/Swiss Festival is usually held at Evian on Lake Geneva in April. In June there is a pairs championship at Chaumont. The

General Secretary of the Swiss Federation, Wolfgang Achterberg, will gladly supply players who are interested with more detailed information. The address is:

Wolfgang Achterberg
Secretaire general FSB
12 Route de Malagnou
1200 Geneva
Switzerland

The Italian Federation is also very active, but so far I believe only Austria and Yugoslavia are well represented in Italian events. For this reason I would like to publicise a wonderful festival in September in Venice on the Lido, another in Rimini in August, and the Cino del Duca Pairs Championship for the Coup d'Or – a unique event which will be held in Milan in May 1972. For detailed information of all events write to:

Federico Rosa
Secretary General
Federazione Italiana Bridge
Largo Augusto 3
20122 Milan
Italy

Holland is, of course, one of my favourite bridge countries. The Dutch welcome visitors with open arms and the bridge is always most interesting. The organisation is first-class, and as they have a busy calendar I would advise you to write to:

N. J. Neelis
Director – Nederlandse Bridge-Bond
Postgiro 22 77 99
Emmapark 9
's-Gravenhage
Holland

In Austria I can recommend above all the Open Pairs event which is held near Vienna in the lovely mountains of the Semmering. Another popular event is usually played in May or June at Velden on the Worthersee in Carinthia. In November there are two popular events, one in Graz and one in Salzburg. Details will gladly be supplied by:

> Mrs Ruth Zohar
> Osterreichischer Bridge-Verband
> Skodagasse 14/16
> 1080 Wein
> Austria

Sweden has what is probably the largest bridge population in Europe, and holds tournaments all the time. Foreign participants are welcomed and details of events may be obtained from the following address:

> Mr Lars Salsby
> General Secretary
> Sveriges Bridgeforbund
> Hollandargatan 9A
> 111 36 Stockholm
> Sweden

The French Bridge Federation (and here I will include Monaco), in liaison with the various tourist offices and casinos, offers many popular events which hardly need advertising, but the outstanding ones are at Cannes in April, Juan-les-Pins in May, Monte Carlo in June, Deauville in July, La Baule in August, Le Touquet in September. The General Secretary of the Federation can be reached at the following address:

> Secretaire General Administratif
> Federation Francaise de Bridge
> 53 Avenue Hoche
> Paris VIII
> France

Portugal has an annual event in the beautiful Algarve in November; details from:

Centro de Bridge de Lisboa
Avenida Antonio Augusto de Aguiar
                                163-4°. Esq.
Lisbon
Portugal

There are also annual events in Morocco, Lebanon, Poland, Germany, Israel and Cairo, and I give the addresses of the various organisations from whom details may be obtained below:

Dirk Schroeder
Deutsche Bridge-Sport-Zentrale
6200 Weisbaden
Adenaurring 36
Germany

Lebanese Bridge Federation
P.O. Box 2481
Beirut
Lebanon

Federation d'Echec et Bridge de la RAU
Gezira Sporting Club
le Caire
RAU

Mme L. Bergé
10 Rue de l'Ourcq
Rabat
Morocco

Dr Bardach
62 La Guardia Street
Tel Aviv
Israel

A. Simon
Krowoderska 56
Krakow
Poland